LEGAL EDUCATION

IN THE

UNITED STATES

By

ALBERT J. HARNO

A Report Prepared for the
Survey of the Legal Profession

GREENWOOD PRESS, PUBLISHERS
WESTPORT, CONNECTICUT

Library of Congress Cataloging in Publication Data

Harno, Albert James, 1889-1966.
Legal education in the United States.

Reprint of the 1953 ed. published by Bancroft-Whitney Co., San Francisco.
Includes index.
1. Law--Study and teaching--United States.
I. Survey of the Legal Profession. II. Title.
[KF273.H27 1980] 340'.07'1173 80-23717
ISBN 0-313-22425-0 (lib. bdg.)

Reprinted in 1980 by Greenwood Press,
A division of Congressional Information Service, Inc.
88 Post Road West, Westport, Connecticut 06881

Printed in the United States of America

10 9 8 7 6 5 4 3 2 1

TABLE OF CONTENTS

†

This book was published for the Survey of the Legal Profession by Bancroft-Whitney Company whose generous assistance and sincere cooperation the Survey Council's Committee on Publications has authorized me gratefully to acknowledge.

REGINALD HEBER SMITH
Director

LEGAL EDUCATION IN THE UNITED STATES

Albert J. Harno*

I. INTRODUCTION

The skills and proficiencies involved in the practice of law are manifold and from this complex stem the problems of legal education. It has been said that the practice of law is an art, and so it is. But is competency in the legal profession to be measured alone by the proved skill of the craftsman? Others have emphasized that the practice of law is a public calling, carrying high ethical responsibilities, and that the profession is a learned one with a vast literature which its votaries must master. This, indeed, is true, but again, is competency on the part of the members of the profession to be measured alone by their achieved learning and their ethical standards? Often the debate over legal education has centered on the relative merits of apprenticeship

* When this study was begun the writer invited a number of individuals, selected from the profession and from the lay public, to advise him on the undertaking. The members of the professional group are: James E. Brenner, Paul W. Brosman, Elliott E. Cheatham, Herbert W. Clark, Lon L. Fuller, Bernard C. Gavit, Frederick D. G. Ribble, Will Shafroth, and Russell N. Sullivan.

Those of the lay group are: B. J. Cahn, President, B. Kuppenheimer & Co., Inc.; Frank G. Dickinson, Director, Bureau of Medical Economic Research, American Medical Association; Robert L. Johnson, President, Temple University; M. G. Kispert, Massachusetts Institute of Technology; Richard L. Kozelka, Dean, University of Minnesota School of Business Administration; and G. Herbert Smith, President, Willamette University.

The writer takes pleasure in acknowledging the many constructive criticisms and the generous helpful advice he has received from these individuals.

as opposed to university training. While the profession has always had some individuals who have spoken with clarity on the subject, the prevailing notions on preparation for law have vacillated from one period of history to another, depending on whether this motif or that was in the ascendancy. The controversy has not ended. Today, when legal education in university law schools is, in the United States, the common route to the profession, one cogent criticism of the schools is that the training they offer is wanting in perspective and breadth of learning, but the most vocal stricture is that it is not practical enough.

A second and related problem of legal education has had to do with the question of standards of admission to the study of law and to the bar. It has involved an extended controversy between advocates of high standards of admission and those who were opposed to such moves. These were not minor skirmishes; they were issues on which strong-minded men spoke with feeling and from conviction. Those favoring standards for admission sought to impress the view that the privilege of practicing law is of high public concern; that the lawyer is the spokesman for others; that in representing others, their property, their liberty, and, indeed, their lives may depend on the breadth of his learning, his knowledge of law, and the skill with which he works; that it follows that the privilege to practice law should be granted only to applicants of proved learning, fitness, and competence.

The position of those who opposed these moves is difficult to define. Their arguments were apparently based on the undeclared major premise that all men have the inherent right to practice law. Explicitly they contended that admittance to the profession must not be denied the "poor boy"; that the practice of law must not become the privilege of the well-to-do; that university and law-school prerequisites create economic barriers to the profession for worthy but indigent young men, and that the imposition of these barriers makes access to it possible only for those of the privileged class. At the present time the impact of this argument has lost much of its force because of the greatly increased opportunities for college and professional education, but the tardiness with which standards of admission were established bears significant testimony to its persuasiveness, and even today it is a formidable obstacle to the raising of standards.

The foregoing are some of the principal factors in the evolution of legal education, but as a river wanders in its course, and has many tributaries, so has been the development of this subject.

II. OUR ENGLISH HERITAGE

A. THE INNS OF COURT

Legal education in the United States had its roots in English history, and in England preparation for the practice of law has been, in the main, through apprenticeship training and through the Inns of Court. This heritage has had a profound effect on the development of legal education in America, on the evolution of our legal institutions, and on our outlook on law. It is true that, when legal education in this country gravitated to the universities, a factor was introduced into the American scene which tended materially to differentiate our system from that of England's and to align the American program with that of the continental countries of Europe where for centuries law had been taught in the universities. But that alignment is more seeming than real. In the great Continental centers of legal learning, law was taught as a science and in the setting of its interrelations with the humanities and the social sciences.[1] The emphasis in English legal education has ever been severely practical.

Thayer in discoursing on the English Bar of the late 1700's

[1] Hazeltine, *Legal Profession and Legal Education, Ancient and Mediaeval*, 9 Encyc. Soc. Sc. 324 (1933); Riesenfeld, *A Comparison of Continental and American Legal Education*, 36 Mich. L. Rev. 31 (1937); Deák, *French Legal Education and Some Reflections on Legal Education in the United States*, 1939 Wis. L. Rev. 473; Schweinburg, Law Training in Continental Europe (Rus. Sage Found.) 14 (1945); Cheatham, *Legal Education in Turkey: Some Thoughts on Education for Foreign Students*, 2 J. Legal Ed. 21 (1949). It must not be taken that the Continental system does not involve practical training. Extended apprenticeships are required after the students have finished their legal studies in the universities. For an instructive article on the Latin-American system, see Horack, *Legal Education in the Latin-American Republics*, 2 J. Legal Ed. 287 (1950).

spoke of the "conservatism of a powerful profession, absorbed in the mere business of its calling, itself untrained in the learned or scientific study of law, and unconscious of the need for such training."[2] Roger North, describing an earlier period, wrote, "Of all the professions in the world, that pretend to book-learning, none is so destitute of institution as that of the common law."[3] Holdsworth deplored the heavy stress the English system laid on the practical aspects of training at the expense of learning, and noted that the "absence of any system of legal education had some very unfortunate effects," during the eighteenth and the early part of the nineteenth century, "upon the government of the state and upon the administration of the law."[4] More recently, Sir David Maxwell-Fyfe, Treasurer of Gray's Inn, in speculating "on the causes of some of the things which may seem peculiarly English to lawyers from the Continent of Europe when they make the acquaintance" of the English legal profession, raised some pertinent questions. "Is our reluctance to codify our law," he queried, "due at all to the old habit of studying it piecemeal by discussions in the evening between those who have spent the day on concrete cases? Is the pride of place which we still give to the judge and the practicing lawyer, as opposed to the professor, in the exposition and development of our law," he went on to inquire, "due to the Inns of Court having for so long been the main fountain of legal education?"[5]

The Inns of Court were and are an amazing institution, without parallel in history. Their evolution presents a fascinating story which cannot be told here except as it relates

[2] *The Teaching of English Law at Universities*, 9 Harv. L. Rev. 169, 171 (1895).

[3] *A Discourse on the Study of the Laws*, quoted, 6 Holdsworth, A History of English Law, 489 (1927).

[4] 12 Holdsworth, *ibid.*, 90 (1938).

[5] *The Inns of Court and the Impact on the Legal Profession in England*, 4 Southwestern L. J. 391, 395–396 (1950).

to the theme of this study.[6] Clearly they have had a tremendous impact on the English legal profession. Their origin is obscured in the mists of history. Holdsworth states that as early as 1292, Edward I directed the judges to make provision for apprentices of the law. He found incidental references to the teaching of law in London in 1293.[7] It was during this period "that these apprentices became organized; and we begin to be able to discern the attorneys, the students, and the barristers of the present day,"[8] and it was in the centuries immediately following that the Inns of Court came into being. Holdsworth places their origin "well back into the fourteenth century."[9] One of the early descriptive accounts of them is by Fortescue, who was a member of Lincoln's Inn, and "a governor of the Inn in 1425, 1426, and 1429."[10] They were, wrote Fortescue,[11]

> "a sort of an Academy, or Gymnasium, fit for persons of their station; where they learn singing, and all kinds of music, dancing and such other accomplishments and diversions . . . At other times, out of term, the greater part apply themselves to the study of the law. Upon festival days, and after the offices of the church are over, they employ themselves to the study of sacred and prophane history: here every thing which is good and virtuous is to be learned: all vice is discouraged and banished . . . The discipline is so excellent, that there is scarce ever known to be any picques or differences, any bickerings or disturbances amongst them."

[6] Much has been written about the Inns. Holdsworth is, of course, a reliable source of information. Another interesting account of them is: Barton, The Story of Our Inns of Court (1924).

[7] 2 Holdsworth, A History of English Law, 314–315 (1923).

[8] *Ibid.*, 493.

[9] *Ibid.*, 494.

[10] *Ibid.*

[11] De Laudibus Legum Angliae, c. 49 (1917 printing).

The Inns of Court reached their highest development in the 1500's. The instruction then given, said Holdsworth,[12] was "eminently well suited to the needs of a youthful system of law, the literature of which was as yet of a manageable size. It was perhaps," he conjectures, "the only system possible for an age in which there was no printed books."[13] The training offered was, in the main, oral. The Inns were governed, as they have been for centuries, by Benchers. The chief instructor was the Reader who was selected by the Benchers. This was an important office, Sir David Maxwell-Fyfe relates, which only rich men could accept, for the Readers "had to give magnificent feasts."[14] It was the duty of the Reader to "make his Reading" which involved an exposition on some branch of the law. Beyond that there were bolts and moots. As described by Sir David,[15]

> "A bolt was a case propounded for argument among the inner barristers and conducted by the outer barristers. A moot (as then practiced) consisted of the putting of a doubtful case by an outer barrister in hall after supper, which was argued by one or two benches. A mimic law suit followed in which inner and outer barristers and benchers took part."

The period of instruction, when the Inns were at their height, was long, as much as 7 or 8 years, and it even reached

[12] 6 Holdsworth, A History of English Law, 481 (1927).

[13] This statement may be open to some reflection in view of the excellent reputation some of the universities on the continent of Europe and elsewhere had then, and had had before that for centuries, for legal scholarship and their programs of legal education, notably the schools in Rome, Beirut, Alexandria, Athens, Bologna, and Paris. Hazeltine, *Legal Profession and Legal Education, Ancient and Mediaeval*, 9 Encyc. Soc. Sc. 324, 326–329 (1933). Ames, *The Vocation of the Law Professor*, in Lectures on Legal History, 354 (1913).

[14] *The Inns of Court and the Impact on the Legal Profession in England*, 4 Southwestern L. J. 391, 393 (1950).

[15] *Ibid.*, 394.

12 years in the Elizabethan days. Later, as the programs of the Inns declined, it became very short. It was, commented Holdsworth, during the golden age of the Inns, "a very practical system—it produced pleaders and advocates; and at the same time theory was not neglected—it produced accomplished lawyers. This system," he goes on to say,

> "was maintained right down to the outbreak of the Great Rebellion. But it had begun to decline in the latter part of the sixteenth century, and it was maintained with increasing difficulty in the earlier half of the seventeenth century. It collapsed during the Commonwealth period; and, in spite of attempts by the Inns of Court and the judges to revive it after the Restoration, it never recovered. By the end of this period the Inns of Court had ceased to be educational bodies; and the student was left to make his own arrangements for his education."[16]

B. WILLIAM BLACKSTONE

One additional chapter from the history of English legal education is to be noted. It was a significant chapter because of the promise it held forth for the English system, and because of the implications it had for the formative period of American legal education. It relates to the appointment in 1753 of William Blackstone as a lecturer on law at Oxford, his later appointment in 1758 as Vinerian professor at Oxford, and the writing, publication and influence of his famous *Commentaries*. Blackstone sought to establish a "system of legal education," and in that he failed. Yet his "life-work, and above all his faith in the necessary alliance between law and letters," said Dicey,[17]

> "have in fact been fruitful of memorable results. Fail-

[16] 6 Holdsworth, A History of English Law, 481 (1927).

[17] *Blackstone's Commentaries*, 4 Camb. L. J. 286, 300 (1932).

ure to create a great school of law in England has been balanced by a triumphant success in the United States, of which Englishmen hardly appreciate the importance. Americans, even before the Thirteen Colonies established their independence, were and have till today continued to be a nation of lawyers; the Constitution of the United States owed its creation, and still owes its maintenance to the fact that the people of America have been thoroughly imbued with the principles, we might even say with the prejudices, of the English common law. Hence the soundness and the extension of legal education is in America a matter which deeply and obviously concerns the welfare of the nation. Now—and this is the matter here to be noted—legal education has in the United States been from the beginning influenced by the work and ideas of Blackstone."[18]

Numerous encomiums have been heaped on Blackstone. His *Commentaries* have been made the subject by many individuals of the highest praise that on occasion has approached adulation. Others, and particularly Bentham, have been devastatingly critical of them. James Fitzjames Stephen has made a brief but discerning appraisal of the man Blackstone and his work.[19] The defects in the *Commentaries,* said he, "are sufficiently obvious. Blackstone was

[18] Holdsworth has commented in a similar vein: "Though Blackstone's attempt to establish a system of legal education then failed, it has had some very important effects. It showed up the evils of the absence of a system of legal education in a manner which assisted the reformers of the nineteenth century; it helped to introduce in America, more quickly than in this country, the public teaching of law; and it gave to the students of English law what they had long needed — a book of Institutes, of such merit that it became at once a legal classic both in England and America." 12 Holdsworth, A History of English Law, 91 (1938).

[19] 2 Stephen, A History of the Criminal Law of England, 214–215 (1883).

neither a profound nor an accurate thinker, and he carried respect for the system which he administered and described to a length which blinded him to its defects, and led him in many instances to write in a tone of courtly, overstrained praise which seems absurd to our generation." But this is not a true measure of Blackstone and his work. Admitting all this, Stephen continues,

> "the fact still remains, that Blackstone first rescued the law of England from chaos. He did, and did exceedingly well, for the end of the eighteenth century, what Coke tried to do, and did exceedingly ill, about 150 years before; that is to say, he gave an account of the law as a whole, capable of being studied, not only without disgust, but with interest and profit."

Stephen wrote in 1883. Today, Blackstone has an important and secure place in legal history. "It appears to us," said Pollock, "that the time has come for editing Blackstone as a historical classic."[20] Dicey[21] and Holdsworth[22] have made similar appraisals. "Blackstone's *Commentaries*," wrote Holdsworth,[23] "are now a recognized legal classic both in England and the United States, so that they may be said to have outlived the speculations of utilitarian law reformers and analytical jurists."

The measure of the stature of Blackstone as an historical figure has significance for this study, but our more immediate interest in him centers on the impact he had on the formative period of legal education in America. And here two factors deserve stress, first, Blackstone's conception of and ideas on the content and scope of legal education and, second, the reception and influence of his *Commentaries* as a text

---

[20] *Notes*, 35 L. Q. Rev. 212 (1919).

[21] *Blackstone's Commentaries*, 4 Camb. L. J. 286 (1932).

[22] 12 Holdsworth, A History of English Law, 702–737 (1938).

[23] *Ibid.*, 736.

used by students in preparing themselves for the practice of law.[24]

When Blackstone began his lectures at Oxford in 1753, legal education in England was at its nadir. It was a period when the only avenue of preparation for the profession was through self-education and office apprenticeships. For the most part the candidates read *Coke on Littleton,* a dull and most difficult undertaking. Lord Hardwicke, in commenting on his experiences as a student, described legal education of that time as a "crabbed barbarous study that has the greatest tendency to make a man unmannerly."[25] Blackstone's lectures at Oxford were an innovation. They were the first lectures on English law ever given in a university. In the initial lecture, *On the Study of the Law,* he described the then deplorable state of affairs relating to legal education, and set forth his conception of a sound system. Much of Blackstone's *Commentaries* is now obsolete, but not this lecture. It is as live today as when he spoke. Blackstone failed in his attempt to establish a system of legal education in England, but his first lecture stands as a beacon in a desolate area. Though he failed in England, his message was transmitted to America, where the *Commentaries,* of which this lecture was a part, were read and digested by numerous students preparing for the practice of law. It was in America, but only after uncertain years of incubation, that it bore results.

In this lecture Blackstone stressed the need of an acquaintance on the part of all citizens with the laws of the land and the urgency for the development of courses on law in the universities. In arguing this point he emphasized an

[24] A good bibliographical catalogue of Blackstone's writings, the various editions of his *Commentaries*, and a listing of notes to his *Commentaries* has been made, Eller, The William Blackstone Collection in the Yale Law Library (1938).

[25] Life of Hardwicke, quoted in 12 Holdsworth, *ibid.*, 89.

objective which unfortunately even today remains unrecognized in our schools and universities. "Let us only reflect a moment," he urged,[26] "on the singular frame and polity of that land, which is governed by this system of laws. A land, perhaps the only one in the universe in which political or civil liberty is the very end and scope of the constitution." Even those of "inferior condition" should know of these laws within the "sphere in which they are appointed to move. But those, on whom nature and fortune have bestowed more abilities and greater leisure, cannot be so easily excused. These advantages are given them," he reasoned,[27] "not for the benefit of themselves only, but also of the public: and yet they cannot, in any scene of life, discharge properly their duty either to the public or themselves, without some degree of knowledge in the laws." He stressed that all individuals should be informed on the law relating to wills and the disposition of their property, and observed[28] that ignorance on this subject "must always be of dangerous consequence, to such as by choice or necessity compile their own testaments without any technical assistance." He said[29] that "those who have attended the courts of justice are the best witnesses of the confusion and distresses that are hereby occasioned in families." Indeed, he went on to say,[30] "it is perfectly amazing, that there should be no other state of life, no other occupation, art, or science, in which some method of instruction is not looked upon as requisite, except only the science of legislation, the noblest and most difficult of any." He argued that all legislators should have an understanding of law, and pointed out that "the mischiefs that have arisen to

[26] 1 Blackstone, Commentaries on the Laws of England, 6 (5th ed. 1773).

[27] *Ibid.*, 7.

[28] *Ibid.*, 7.

[29] *Ibid.*, 7.

[30] *Ibid.*, 9.

the public from inconsiderate alterations in our laws, are too obvious to be called in question," and stressed that the extent to which these mischiefs "have been owing to the defective education of our senators, is a point well worthy the public attention."[31] Knowledge so essential to all, he contended, can best be taught in the universities. That a "science like this should have ever been deemed unnecessary to be studied in a university," he concluded,[32] "is a matter of astonishment and concern."

After outlining his thesis on a course in law for all students, Blackstone then proceeded to state his views on a program of education for law students. He noted the decline, as educational institutions, of the Inns of Court, and the absence, in the English system of his day, of any program of formal education for the prospective lawyer. This "want of some assistance in the rudiments of legal knowledge," he pointed out, had given rise to some pernicious consequences. "I mean," said he, "the custom, by some so very warmly recommended, of dropping all liberal education, as of no use to students in the law: and placing them, in its stead, at the desk of some skilful attorney; in order to initiate them early in all the depths of practice, and render them more dextrous in the mechanical part of business."[33] Some, to be sure, he observed, had become excellent lawyers, "in spight of this method of education," and this had "afforded some kind of sanction to this illiberal path to the profession." However, after making "due allowance," he went on to say,[34]

> "for one or two shining exceptions, experience may teach us to fortell that a lawyer thus educated to the bar, in subservience to attorneys and solicitors, will find he has begun at the wrong end . . . And what the conse-

[31] *Ibid.*, 10.
[32] *Ibid.*, 27.
[33] *Ibid.*, 31, 32.
[34] *Ibid.*, 32, 33.

quence may be, to have the interpretation and enforcement of the laws (which include the entire disposal of our properties, liberties, and lives) fall wholly into the hands of obscure or illiterate men, is a matter of very public concern."

He argued that these "inconveniences" can never "be effectually prevented, but by making academical education a previous step to the profession of the common law, and at the same time making the rudiments of the law a part of academical education."[35] With rare discernment he then proceeded to outline how law should be taught in the universities. The "expounder of the laws," said he,[36]

> "should consider his course as a general map of the law, marking out the shape of the country, its connexions and boundaries, its greater divisions and principal cities: it is not his business to describe minutely the subordinate limits, or to fix the longitude and latitude of every inconsiderable hamlet. His attention should be engaged, like that of the readers in Fortescue's inns of chancery, 'in tracing out the originals and as it were the elements of the law.' . . . These originals should be traced to their fountains, as well as our distance will permit; to the customs of the Britons and Germans, as recorded by Caesar and Tacitus; to the codes of the northern nations on the continent, and more especially to those of our own Saxon princes; to the rules of the Roman law . . .; but, above all, to that inexhaustible reservoir of legal antiquities and learning, the feodal law, or, as Spelman has entitled it, the law of nations in our western orb. These primary rules and fundamental principles should be weighed and compared with the precepts of the law of nature, and the practice of other

[35] *Ibid.*, 33.

[36] *Ibid.*, 35–36.

countries; should be explained by reasons, illustrated by examples, and confirmed by undoubted authorities; their history should be deduced, their changes and revolutions observed, and it should be shewn how far they are connected with, or have at any time been affected by, the civil transactions of the kingdom."

C. INFLUENCE OF THE ENGLISH SYSTEM IN AMERICA

From the premises of the English scheme of legal education may we now pause for a brief appraisal of some of the implications the English system has had for America. No American institution, excepting perhaps the field of literature, bears so close a tie to a corresponding English institution as does the law. The structure of American law is erected on the foundations of the English common law. The common law is judge-made law and as such it is a series of judicial decisions. Whatever the merits of the common law may be, and there are many, symmetry, except in a sprawling sort of way, is not one of them. We can conjecture here that intimate association with and schooling in this system of law accounts in no small measure for the resistance of the English bar to law codification. We can make a similar conjecture as to the attitude of the American bar on this subject. It follows that the conception of legal education held by English lawyers was engendered by the legal system within which they worked. Under the common law the attention of English lawyers centered on what the judges said and did, and, even more important, on how they were likely to decide a case currently in dispute. This tended to focus their interest on particulars and to draw them away from deliberations on the broader contexts and implications of the law.

In these surroundings the notions of English lawyers on how law was to be learned were developed. It had to be learned through the study of particulars and through action. This, in turn, tends to explain the skepticism of the English relative to the teaching of law in the universities and their extreme emphasis on office-apprenticeship training. Herein lies the reason for the failure of Blackstone's great experiment.

In America, as we shall see, legal education until well past the middle of the 1800's followed the English pattern. In the late 1700's and early 1800's several chairs of law, in the tradition of Blackstone's chair at Oxford, were founded in American universities. The able men who occupied them had a broad conception of legal education as a part of a liberal education. The establishment of these chairs was an event in the history of American legal education. It carried into effect in America what Blackstone had so eloquently advocated for the education of the English bar. It focused attention in America on the need for and the benefits of a liberal education for lawyers, but once more, here in America as in England, this was a design that came to naught. With the advent of Christopher Columbus Langdell and the initiation of the case method of study in the early 1870's, a more dramatic and revolutionary movement in legal education was in the making.

The case method will be discussed later. Here it may suffice to point out that while it is pursued in the universities under the guidance of full-time law teachers, as distinguished from the office apprenticeships of the English system, and to that extent is a fulfillment of Blackstone's proposal, it tends otherwise to be a restriction on the broader implications of Blackstone's conception. The case method ushered in a new era in legal education. It did more than that; it marked an epoch in teaching methodology in the broad area of American education. What is of note for us here, however, is that this development, while a highly valuable contribution to teaching and learning, was in the tradition of the common law. In a real sense it was a return to the system of education pursued in the Inns of Court when they were at their heyday in the Middle Ages. The case method as originally conceived was restricted to the study of judge-made law. It isolated students from the study of all else; adjudicated cases were the exclusive sources of law with which the students dealt. This was a scheme of education that could only have been nurtured in the soil of the common law, and it was severely limited to that source. It is true that the case method of study, as conceived in America, was a vast improvement over its English prototype, but it was in the pattern of the English system. Thayer has given us an accurate description. "We, in America," said he,[37]

> "have carried legal education much farther than it has gone in England. There the systematic teaching of law in schools is but faintly developed. Here it is elaborate, widely favored, rapidly extending. Why is this? Not because we originated this method. We transplanted an English root, and nurtured and developed it, while at home it was suffered to languish and die down."

[37] *The Teaching of English Law at Universities*, 9 Harv. L. Rev. 169, 169–170 (1895).

III. THE FORMATIVE PERIOD OF AMERICAN LEGAL EDUCATION

A. THE COLONIAL PERIOD

A social consciousness of the significance of law to a people is an attribute of a ripening civilization. There was no conceptual legal system in early Colonial America, and no legal profession. The Colonists' feeling toward lawyers was not merely negative; they viewed lawyers with suspicion and distrust. Several factors contributed to this attitude. First, it was a reaction that is characteristic of a pioneer country. Also the Colonists did not carry with them from the homeland happy memories of the profession, and the few individuals who posed as "attorneys" in the Colonies did not increase their respect for it. They "were at first mostly pettifoggers, or minor court officers such as deputy sheriffs, clerks and justices, who stirred up litigation for the sake of the petty court fees."[1] The growth of the profession was slow. There were few lawyers in the Colonies before the 1700's and it was not until the latter part of that century that they began to assume a place of influence in public affairs and in the consciousness of the people.[2] In the dramatic days of the Revolution and in the years immediately following, lawyers occupied a place of extreme importance. The work of lawyers during those fateful years, in the contributions they made in ideas and services to the welfare of the Republic, constitutes one of the most glorious chapters in the history of the nation.

Preparation for the practice of law in early Colonial America was desultory. What colleges there were did

[1] Warren, A History of the American Bar, 5 (1911).

[2] Brown, Lawyers and the Promotion of Justice, 11 (1938).

not offer courses in law and there were no independent law schools. Some individuals made scanty preparation for the practice through serving as copyists or assistants in the offices of the clerks of court. A few went to England to the Inns of Court, but as we have seen, the Inns had little of substance to offer them. For the most part, preparation was through apprenticeships in the offices of members of the bar, for which privilege the apprentice paid a fee. Warren quotes an interesting bit of concrete evidence on that subject:[3]

> "Phila. March 22, 1782. I promise to pay James Wilson Esq. or order on demand one hundred guineas, his fee for receiving my nephew Bushrod Washington as a student of law in his office. G. Washington."

The prospects before the aspirant to the profession as to the materials from which he might gain an education were not encouraging. Law books were extremely scarce. Only about thirty English reports of a total of one hundred fifty then published were in common use in the Colonies at the time of the Revolution. The number of available textbooks was even smaller. The colleges had no law books and only the more affluent lawyers possessed libraries, consisting of reports and texts, of from fifty to one hundred volumes. A common reading assignment for the young apprentice was Coke's *Institutes*, a work well characterized as that "disorderly mass of crabbed pedantry that Coke poured forth as institutes of English law."[4] The student read *Coke on Littleton, Bracton, Britton, Fleta* and *Glanville*.[5] That the study of law through mediums of that sort would produce lawyers of limited knowledge and perspec-

[3] A History of the American Bar, 166 (1911).

[4] Quoted by Thayer, *The Teaching of English Law at Universities*, 9 Harv. L. Rev. 169, 179 (1895).

[5] Warren, A History of the American Bar, 173 (1911).

tive is not a subject for wonder; the matter for wonder arises over the fact that some few individuals thus schooled could transcend the bondage of their tutelage and become men of breadth of learning and vision.

Judge Story has given us an account of his first experiences. After leaving college, Story entered the office of Samuel Sewall, a distinguished lawyer in Massachusetts. Sewall told Story to read *Coke on Littleton.* "It was a very large folio," related Story,[6]

> "with Hargrave and Butler's notes, which I was required to read also. Soon after his [Sewall's] departure, I took it up, and after trying it day after day with very little success, I sat myself down and wept bitterly. My tears dropped upon the book, and stained its pages."

Daniel Webster also has given us a statement on his impressions. After finishing college he entered the office of Thomas W. Thompson, a neighbor of Webster's father. Thompson believed that students should learn law by reading the hardest book first and assigned *Coke on Littleton.* Webster later expressed his disapproval of that practice. "A boy of twenty," said he,[7]

> "with no previous knowledge of such subjects, cannot understand Coke. It is folly to set him upon such an author. There are propositions in Coke so abstract, and distinctions so nice, and doctrines embracing so many distinctions and qualifications, that it requires an effort not only of a mature mind, but of a mind both strong and mature, to understand him. Why disgust and discourage a young man by telling him he must break into his profession through such a wall as this?"

---

[6] Story, *Autobiography*, in Miscellaneous Writings, 1, 20 (1852).

[7] 1 The Works of Daniel Webster, *Biographical Memoir*, 11th ed. xxviii (1858).

B. THE TRANSITION PERIOD

It should be noted that when Judge Story and Daniel Webster were law students, a transition in American legal education was well in the making. The reading of *Coke on Littleton* by neophyte lawyers, to be sure, was to continue for some years. What challenges our interest is that in the latter part of the 1700's and early 1800's the profession was in a ferment which was to result in a truly remarkable change in the attitude and outlook of lawyers toward law, and toward legal education. Lawyers in number seemed suddenly to cast off the mental confinement associated with the routines of the practice of law and to become enlightened leaders in public affairs. It was one of those periods in history which are difficult to account for, and we can do little more than conjecture about it.

It was a time of stirring events, but history has recorded other periods when momentous social, economic or political problems were brewing and which were followed by tragic consequences because of a dearth of great leaders to solve them. Much that contributed to this period of enlightenment must be attributed to the reading of great books. Blackstone's *Commentaries* were widely read and their influence was substantial. Pound has pointed out that Blackstone's section "on the nature of laws in general" was founded on Grotius and Pufendorf. John Adams and others read the works of these men. Burlamaqui's *Principles of Natural and Politic Law* had been translated and was read by many. Webster, after his experiences in the office of Mr. Thompson, took up his studies with Christopher Gore, a distinguished lawyer and statesman. In Gore's office Webster read some of the best authors of the time, including Vattel.[8] Kent listed among his readings, Black-

[8] Webster later made effective use of Vattel, 5 The Works of Daniel Webster, 392–394 (1858).

stone, Grotius, Pufendorf and Hume's History.[9] Judge Simeon E. Baldwin has mentioned, in addition, among the books commonly read during that period, Montesquieu, and the Institutes of Justinian. "Whatever else might be omitted," said Baldwin, "in any case, Blackstone's *Commentaries* never were."[10] "We must remember," commented Pound, "that these books and others of the sort were the staple of the beginnings of American legal education."[11]

It should not be taken, however, that legal education, in this extraordinary era, had developed into an ordered system. The education of most lawyers of that time was pathetically superficial. What is noteworthy is that a few lawyers were remarkably well educated and enlightened, and they became the professional and public leaders of their time. These men took for granted that the study of law, government, and society formed one seamless web.[12] To them law, economics, politics, and sociology were parts of a synthesis. Here was a group of exceptional men who in their schooling had come under the influence of great minds, and whose thinking was stimulated and shaped by those experiences. The fountainhead of this development was Blackstone. "It was the advent of Blackstone," wrote Warren,[13] "which opened the eyes of American scholars to the broader field of learning in the law. He taught them, for the first time, the continuity, the unity, and the reason of the Common Law—and just at a time when the need of a unified system both in law and politics was beginning to be felt in the Colonies." It was Blackstone's great experiment in the teaching of law in a university, said

---

[9] Memoirs and Letters, 19 (1898).

[10] *The Study of Elementary Law*, 13 Yale L. J. 1, 2–3 (1903).

[11] The Formative Era of American Law, 24 (1938).

[12] Preliminary Statement of the Committee on Legal Education of the Harvard Law School, 92 (1947).

[13] A History of the American Bar, 177 (1911).

Thayer,[14] "and the publication, a little before the American Revolution, of the results of that experiment, which furnished the stimulus and the exemplar for our own early attempts at systematic legal education."

C. THE ESTABLISHMENT OF CHAIRS OF LAW

One immediate effect traceable to Blackstone's influence was the establishment of chairs of law in several American colleges and universities. "With the close of the Revolutionary War," said Warren,[15] "there began a new era in legal education." Under the guiding hand of Thomas Jefferson[16] a chair of law was founded in 1779 at William and Mary College with George Wythe as the first incumbent. Some of Wythe's students became distinguished lawyers, among them John Marshall and St. George Tucker. When Wythe resigned his professorship in 1789, Tucker was appointed to succeed him. Tucker taught law in the Blackstone tradition, basing his lectures on Blackstone's *Commentaries,* supplemented with Tucker's own notes on American law. These notes became the materials for an annotated edition of Blackstone, which Tucker published in 1803. William and Mary College maintained this professorship until 1861.[17]

Within the course of a few years similar professorships were established in other American universities. In 1779, the same year that a chair of law was founded in William and Mary College, Isaac Royall made a will under the

[14] *The Teaching of English Law at Universities,* 9 Harv. L. Rev. 169, 170 (1895).

[15] A History of the American Bar, 341 (1911).

[16] Jefferson was not an admirer of Blackstone. Waterman, *Thomas Jefferson and Blackstone's Commentaries,* 27 Ill. L. Rev. 629, 634 (1933).

[17] Reed, Training for the Public Profession of the Law, 116–117 (Carneg. Found. Bul. 15, 1921).

terms of which he gave property to Harvard College for a professorship of law. Royall died in 1781 but the position was not filled until 1815 when Chief Justice Isaac Parker of Massachusetts was appointed.[18] In 1790 James Wilson, associate justice of the United States Supreme Court, was made professor of law at the College of Philadelphia, but after two years his lectures were discontinued.[19] Transylvania University, Lexington, Kentucky, followed in 1799 with the setting up of a professorship in law and politics. To the honored names of men who held early American professorships of law, observed Ames,[20] "should be added that of Henry Clay, who . . . was for two years professor of law at Transylvania University."

In 1816 the University of Maryland established a professorship of law and appointed David Hoffman to the position. Hoffman with great industry worked out a curriculum which was published under the title, *A Course of Legal Study.*[21] This work received high praise and was characterized by Story[22] as containing "by far the most perfect system for the study of the law which has ever been offered to the public." The course was organized under thirteen separate titles, including *Moral and Political Philosophy, The Law of Nations, Political Economy* and the more orthodox legal subjects. It "embraced a reading of the Bible, Cicero, Seneca, Aristotle, Paley, Adam Smith, Burlamaqui, Montesquieu,

[18] Royall's will, in fact, was dated May 26, 1778. A codicil to this will was drafted November 31, 1779. The codicil provided that the land devised "be appropriated towards the endowing of a Professor of Laws in said College or a Professor of Physics and Anatomy." 1 Warren, History of the Harvard Law School, 281 (1908).

[19] Hurst, The Growth of American Law, 258 (1950).

[20] *The Vocation of the Law Professor*, in Lectures on Legal History, 354, 359 (1913).

[21] Reed, Training for the Public Profession of the Law, 123–126 (Carneg. Found. Bul. 15, 1921).

[22] Miscellaneous Writings, 91 (1852).

and Grotius."[23] It is not what Hoffman accomplished as a teacher that is of note, for his teaching was interrupted shortly after he began lecturing through the seizure of the property of the university by the state. What draws attention to his program is the insight it gives us into the aspirations of the legal educators of that period. It is as if they were moved by a feeling of mission—"a sense of embarking on an adventure in democratic government, an intense desire to seek out the underlying principles that make a satisfactory life in common possible, a faith that the basic problems of law and government can be solved by reason."[24]

With these "honored names," to borrow Ames' description of the men who held professorships during this era, we must include that of James Kent, for Kent, with the possible exception of Story, who really belongs to a somewhat later period, was the most distinguished of them all. Kent was appointed professor of law in Columbia College in 1793, and resigned that position in 1797. Then followed a distinguished public and judicial career. In 1823 he was re-elected professor of law in Columbia College and resumed giving his lectures. It was in this latter period that he conceived the idea of writing a treatise on American law. His lectures were the basis for his famous *Commentaries on American Law.* Kent at a very young age became an admirer of Blackstone. "When the college was broken up and dispersed in July, 1779, by the British," he wrote in his *Memoranda,*[25] "I retired to a country village, and, finding Blackstone's *Commentaries,* I read the four volumes. Parts of the work struck my taste, and the work inspired me, at the age of 15, with awe, and I fondly

[23] Preliminary Statement of the Committee on Legal Education of the Harvard Law School, 94 (1947).

[24] *Ibid.*

[25] Memoirs and Letters of James Kent, 18 (1898).

determined to be a lawyer." Kent, said Pound,[26] "affected the development of the law in three ways: as a judge, by decisions; as a writer, by his institutional treatise that still stands by the side of Blackstone; and as a teacher." If one were to venture, he went on to say,[27] "to assign to individuals some real place in the making of our legal system, I suppose all would agree that three names stand out before all others, namely Marshall, Kent and Story."

Kent, indeed, was one of the molders of American law, and he is a towering figure in the history of legal education and in the history of the legal profession. He was a professor of law, but his reputation rests not on his distinction as a teacher. It is founded on the product of his teaching. Kent's lectures were the beginnings of Kent's *Commentaries*. In many ways Kent's career parallels that of Blackstone. And herein lie the materials for a story that is yet to be written. When in the ripeness of time the history of legal education is written, one inspiring chapter will surely deal with the law teacher as a systematizer and maker of the law. The fact is, though it has not yet been fully recognized, the legal profession for many years, and increasingly, has looked to the law teacher to guide and lead it in matters of legal scholarship.

In the early professorships of law we are dealing with one of the directive forces in the history of legal education. This era signified a departure from the unqualified method of office-apprenticeship training. The practice of law is a craft, and the lawyer should be a good craftsman of the law, but to the men who conceived these professorships, the practice of law was more than a craft. There was need that the lawyer also be a statesman of the law.

---

[26] *The Place of Judge Story in the Making of American Law*, 48 Am. L. Rev. 676, 678 (1914).

[27] *Ibid.*

"History," said Justice Cardozo,[28] "in illuminating the past, illuminates the present, and in illuminating the present, illuminates the future." This was a period in history that is highly illuminative, for in this era men lived and worked who had a thoroughly enlightened conception of the place of law in an ordered and democratic society, and who were sensitive to the fact that this perceptive understanding had to be predicated on the foundation of a broad and liberal educational program for prospective lawyers. It is true, as Pound has pointed out,[29] that the lectures projected by these early teachers "were not and were not meant to be professional training in law." The educational route to the practice of law was then, as it was to be for some time yet to come, through office apprenticeships, and those who attended these lectures were not relieved from traveling that route. The significance of these courses was that they were conceived to lay a broad foundation for the further education of prospective lawyers, and as such they were conceived to be an integral part of a program of legal education.[30] Also, it seems probable, as Ames has conjectured,[31] "that these professorships were created with the hope that they would soon expand into university schools of law."

But just as it seemed that these courses were well-launched in the American scene of legal education, there occurred an hiatus. Over the long view these early ventures were tremendously significant, but in their immediate impact they were failures. "The hopes that may have

[28] The Nature of the Judicial Process, 53 (1928).

[29] *The Law School and the Professional Tradition,* 24 Mich. L. Rev. 156, 160 (1925).

[30] Currie, *The Materials of Law Study,* 3 J. Legal Ed. 331, 357 (1951).

[31] *The Vocation of the Law Professor,* in Lectures on Legal History, 354, 359 (1913).

been entertained," said Ames,[32] "of developing schools of law out of these professorships were in the main doomed to disappointment." Disruptive forces were beginning to take shape in the early part of the 1800's which were to divert the course of legal education from that projected by these pioneer teachers, and it was not until the beginning of the present century that views such as they held were again expressed. Before proceeding, however, with the main movements of legal education, it is apropos that we take cognizance of two parallel but related developments that had to do with the establishment of law schools independent of university affiliation and with early efforts to set up standards of admission to the bar.

D. THE LITCHFIELD SCHOOL

The independent law school, which was to have an important place in the evolution of legal education, was the offspring of the office-apprenticeship system. The first American law school had no university affiliation and was of this type. Ames has given us a striking verbal picture of that first school. "On a broad shaded street in one of the most beautiful of New England villages," in his descriptive words,[33]

> "stands an attractive old Colonial house, the residence, at the close of the American Revolution, of a Connecticut lawyer. Hard by the house was the owner's law office, a small one-story wooden building much resembling the familiar district schoolhouse. There was nothing about it to catch the eye, but it has a peculiar interest for the lawyer, as the birthplace of the American Law School. For it was to this building that young men came from all parts of the country to listen

[32] *Ibid.*

[33] *Ibid.*, 354.

> to the lectures of Judge Reeve, the founder of the celebrated Litchfield Law School."

The Litchfield Law School was in existence for nearly fifty years, from 1784 to 1833.

The time of its beginning is ordinarily given as 1784. In truth, it is difficult to fix the opening date. Sometime between 1774 and 1784 a transition occurred from office-apprenticeship training to the operation of a law school. Tapping Reeve, a Princeton graduate, had gone into the practice of law in Litchfield in 1772. Into Reeve's office in 1774 to study law under him came his brother-in-law, Aaron Burr. Other apprentices entered his office to study with him. In 1782 Reeve departed from the informality of office instruction, and prepared a series of lectures.[34] In 1784 he erected the "small one-story wooden building" mentioned by Ames.

In 1795 James Gould, who had begun his apprenticeship training in the office of another attorney, entered the Litchfield School. Three years later when Reeve was appointed to a judgeship, a partnership for the operation of the School was formed between Reeve and Gould. Gould was an able teacher and administrator and under his guidance the School had its greatest development. Attendance usually varied from nine to thirty students. In 1813 it reached its peak enrollment of fifty-five. When Gould became associated with Reeve in 1798, a simple registration system was established under which each student on entrance to the school wrote his name and the state of his residence in the Register. The Register when the school closed in 1833 listed 805 names. Former students later estimated that 1015 individuals had, over the entire existence of the School, studied law there. The teaching program was

---

[34] Fisher, Litchfield Law School, Yale Law Library Publications, 1 (1946).

divided into forty-eight subjects. Instruction was through lectures lasting approximately an hour and a half a day. Students were required to take careful notes on these lectures, to do collateral reading, and to transcribe their notes into permanent notebooks. Moot courts, optional for the students, were also conducted. The full course extended over fourteen months, which included two vacations of four weeks each. While school was in session, examinations were held every Saturday on the work of the week.[35]

Legal education in this, the first American law school, thus had its origin in "purely practical needs and considerations." It was, as Redlich has pointed out,[36] "exclusively a creation of practitioners." Other law schools, privately operated and of a similar type, soon sprang up but most of them were short-lived and none achieved the reputation of the Litchfield School. "The significance of this group of schools in our educational development," said Reed,[37] "is that they served temporarily to bridge the gap between the students who wished systematized instruction in law and the colleges that were not yet prepared to give it." That, perhaps, was their instant significance, but, over the long view, the establishment of these schools had broader implications, for while the Litchfield School and its immediate imitators had only short existence, they were the precursors of the proprietary law schools of a later period. This type of school was subsequently to undergo various changes—from undertakings operated privately by lawyers, to institutions controlled by non-profit

[35] *Ibid.*, 1–2; Reed, Training for the Public Profession of the Law, 128–132 (Carneg. Found. Bul. 15, 1921).

[36] The Common Law and the Case Method in American University Law Schools, 7 (Carneg. Found. Bul. 8, 1914).

[37] Training for the Public Profession of the Law, 133 (Carneg. Found. Bul. 15, 1921).

corporations; from schools which students attended more or less casually, to degree-awarding institutions. They were the forerunners of a class of night schools some of which are still in operation.

The Litchfield Law School claims our interest not only because it was the first American law school and because it was the exemplar of a class of schools, but because of its students who later achieved distinction. The precept "by their fruits ye shall know them" has come to us through the ages. If judged by no other standard than its "fruits," this School has a distinguished place in the history of legal education. Samuel H. Fisher has compiled a biographical catalogue of the men who attended the School.[38] Of the 903 men listed by him, 28 became United States senators; 101 members of Congress; 34 state supreme court justices; 14 governors of states and 10 lieutenant governors; 3 vice-presidents of the United States; 3 United States Supreme Court justices; and 6 members of the Cabinet. In addition, many on this list became prominent clergymen, businessmen, inventors, editors, and authors. "Perhaps no Law School has had—perhaps I may add ever will have," observed Professor Joel Parker,[39]

> "so great a proportion of distinguished men on its catalogue, if for no other reason, because attendance upon a Law School was then the rare exception, an advantage attained in general only by very ambitious young men, and because there was then much less competition for the offices and honors to which they aspired."

It may be that Professor Parker has given the only possible

[38] Litchfield Law School, Yale Law Library Publications, 9–141 (1946).

[39] The Law School, Harvard College, 8 (1871), quoted by: Brown, Lawyers and the Promotion of Justice, 27 (1938); Warren, A History of the American Bar, 359 (1911).

explanation for the remarkable record of the Litchfield School. Unquestionably any school which over a period of years is substantially recruited with talented and ambitious students will in the course of time have a proud list of distinguished alumni. Yet this does not wholly account for the record of the School. May we conjecture that the physical and intellectual environment in which the Litchfield students worked may have been a contributing factor? "It is easy to see," commented the *Albany Law Journal* in 1879,[40]

> "that the student in the Litchfield Law School had nothing to do but to *learn the law*. The isolated location of the village—in those days when the cities of Hartford and New Haven were distant a day's journey—the absence of any facilities for wasting time in amusement; in short, the quiet and seclusion of a small country village furnished opportunities for study, and impediments to every thing *but* study, which never can be found in law schools established in large cities, as is universally the case now."

Even more credible, perhaps, is the surmise that the students in the Litchfield School were brought into communion with great minds. Is it, perhaps, significant that Judge Reeve graduated from Princeton at the head of his class; that James Gould was a Yale graduate; and that both of these men were superior legal scholars? The probability is that a number of factors worked in salutary combination to make the Litchfield Law School the unique institution it was.

E. THE DEVELOPMENT OF BAR ADMISSION REQUIREMENTS

One observation which over the long view registers repeatedly relates to the sensitive relations between bar admis-

[40] *The Litchfield Law School,* 20 Albany L. J. 72, 73 (1879).

sion requirements and the development of legal education. The history of legal education and that of bar admissions are, indeed, phases of the same story. The Colonial lawyer had little professional consciousness and was apathetic on the question of admission to the practice. Correspondingly the cause of legal education lagged. With the deepening insight during the period just before and after the American Revolution as to the place and function of the lawyer in the social context, the conception of how the lawyer should be educated likewise showed a transformation. Gradually the feeling developed that the profession was and by the very nature of the calling had to be a learned one. By 1770 there were evidences of a growing sense of professional solidarity and responsibility[41] which found expression in the setting up of regulations bearing on the preparation for the practice. Several jurisdictions adopted measures of this sort, some by court rules, some by legislation, and some by action of the organized bar.

At least seventeen jurisdictions adopted regulations in the period between 1767 and 1829. In the main, these regulations established requirements of from three to five years of preparation for admission to the lower courts, and additional requirements, ordinarily two years, for admission to the higher courts. Some jurisdictions made distinctions between attorneys and counsellors; for admission as counsellor the period of preparation was longer. Several required a shorter period of preparation for college graduates. In New Jersey the applicant, beyond meeting the requirements of a period of study, had to pass an examination. In New Hampshire a rule was established that no member of the bar could at one time receive more than three students into his office. "These rigorous requirements," observed

[41] Reed, Training for the Public Profession of the Law, 82–84 (Carneg. Found. Bul. 15, 1921); Warren, A History of the American Bar, 196–203 (1911).

Reed,[42] "were the product of a political philosophy which took no thought of anything save the moral character and the competency of its lawyers."

Stated perhaps more comprehensively, these regulations evidenced an awakening sense of the profession's responsibility to the public—the dawning of the perception that not all men are qualified to practice law; that the lawyer has to be a person of good character and has to meet at least minimum standards of professional competency. They were the forerunners of other and more extensive moves of this sort of a later period, aimed to establish requirements for admission to the bar. In their immediate influence, however, they came to grief, for they were, in the main, swept away by the political and social upsurge of Jacksonian "democracy."

---

[42] Present-Day Law Schools in the United States and Canada, 5 (Carneg. Found. Bul. 21, 1928).

IV. EARLY AMERICAN LAW SCHOOLS AND THE LAISSEZ FAIRE PERIOD

A. The Royall Professorship of Law at Harvard — Justice Parker

In 1779 Isaac Royall made a will endowing a professorship of law in Harvard College. Although Royall died in 1781, this position was not filled until 1815 when Isaac Parker, Chief Justice of the Supreme Judicial Court of Massachusetts, was elected.[1] Under the conditions of his appointment, Parker was required to deliver fifteen lectures for the benefit of college seniors and resident graduates on

> "the theory of law in its most comprehensive sense; the principles and practical operation of the Constitution and Government of the United States and this Commonwealth; a history of the jurisprudence of this State under the Colonial and Provincial as well as under the present government; an explanation of the principles of the Common Law of England, the mode of its introduction into this country, and the sources and reasons of its obligation therein; also the various modifications by usage, judicial decision, and Statute; and, generally, those topics connected with law as a science which will best lead the minds of students to such inquiries and researches as will qualify them to become useful and distinguished supporters of our free system of government, as well as able and honorable advocates of the rights of the citizen."[2]

This was, of course, a laudable assignment, but it was an

---

[1] 1 Warren, History of the Harvard Law School, 278–292 (1908).

[2] Quoted in Warren, *ibid*, 293. Also, Reed, Training for the Public Profession of the Law, 137 (Carneg. Found. Bul. 15, 1921).

undertaking that no one person in the course of a few lectures could encompass. Also, it did not embrace the essentials of a legal education, and no one was more sensitive to that than Parker himself. His inaugural address, reminiscent of Blackstone's first lecture, is a landmark in the history of legal education, for in it he foreshadowed the establishment of the Harvard Law School.

He spoke of the "publick neglect of so important a branch of education." His assignment at Harvard College, he said, was "like all incipient institutions" which "must be imperfect in the outset," but it was undertaken in the hope that it would "grow into a system, honorable to the University and highly useful to the publick." He noted the "present improved condition" of jurisprudence, the respectable standing of the recent generation of lawyers, and contrasted the status of the law and lawyers then with that of an earlier period. "For the first century of our history," he observed, "we learn little of law and lawyers, but the simplicity of one and the insignificance of the other." The profession, he said, "was probably followed by men of low minds and lower reputation, whose efforts were limited to the mechanical drudgery of the craft." A change of insight and attitude was now evident. With the advent of a new generation of lawyers, law "as understood and administered by them" was a "comprehensive system of human wisdom." Law had become a science that merited instruction in a university. "A science like this," he stressed, "is worthy to be taught, for it cannot be understood without instruction." Finally, and this was to be of particular significance for the future of legal education, he proposed that "a school for the instruction of resident graduates in jurisprudence" be "ingrafted on this professorship." He spoke with approval of the Litchfield Law School and expressed the hope that the school he was envisaging would be a "respectable institution of this sort," with the difference that this one would be connected with a university. He emphasized both theoretical and practical training. Students were to study under capable instruction in the law school before they entered "into the office of a counsellor to obtain a knowledge of practice." A program of education of this type and scope, he doubted not, would "tend greatly to improve the character of the Bar of our State."[3]

To Parker goes the credit of envisaging and founding the Harvard Law School. The School became a reality in 1817 and, in addition to Parker, Asahel Stearns was appointed professor. This, indeed, was an event in the history of legal education, but as an educator Parker's perception was limited. His thinking appears not to have extended beyond the immediate demands of the practitioner. The place of professional skills in the training of a lawyer must never be underrated, for it is through expertness of touch that knowledge finds its true expression. But knowledge and discernment are of the essence. The educational program set up by Parker lacked both substance and vision. This, perhaps, is surprising in view of the familiar understanding leaders of the bar of that day had of the writings of great legal scholars. "For the first dozen years of its existence," observed Ames,[4] "the Harvard School was a languishing local institution."

B. OTHER SCHOOLS

As early as 1777 President Ezra Stiles of Yale had drafted a plan for a professorship of law at Yale College, but nothing immediate was done about his proposal. In 1801 Elizur Goodrich was appointed professor of law and served in that

---

[3] Warren, *ibid.*, 299–302. In these pages Warren reproduces substantial portions of Parker's address.

[4] *The Vocation of the Law Professor*, in Lectures on Legal History, 354, 359 (1913).

capacity until 1810.[5] In 1800 a private law school had been opened in New Haven which continued to operate until 1824, at which time Judge David Daggett was made its head. Daggett was promptly appointed to the vacant professorship of law at Yale and in 1826, under his leadership, the Yale Law School came into being. Yale, in fact, adopted the private New Haven law school.[6]

In 1825 Thomas Jefferson, who had been responsible for the establishment, in 1779, of a chair of law at William and Mary College, was able to advance his educational aims yet further through the opening of the University of Virginia, and in 1826 a chair of Law and Politics was filled in that University through the appointment of John T. Lomax.[7]

The precedent having been established, other universities followed and also founded law schools. By 1860 over a score of law schools with university affiliations were in operation.[8] Several of these ventures were short-lived; many that attained permanent standing were in session intermittently before reaching that status; some, e.g., Columbia University and the University of Pennsylvania, had previously founded professorships of law that had ceased to exist. These were not distinguished schools. Though affiliated with universities, the instruction they offered was, in the main "like that at Litchfield, little more than an expanded form of office apprenticeship training,"[9] and not one that was in operation contemporaneously with the Litchfield School enjoyed at that time the favorable reputation of that School. What is notable about this period

[5] Warren, A History of the American Bar, 364 (1911); Reed, Training for the Public Profession of the Law, 136 (Carneg. Found. Bul. 15, 1921).

[6] Reed, *ibid.*, 140–142.

[7] *Ibid.*, 118–119.

[8] *Ibid.*, 423–430.

[9] Hurst, The Growth of American Law, 260 (1950).

is that, at long last, law schools were being operated under the aegis of universities. The decisive step had been taken.

C. BARRIERS TO DEVELOPMENT OF LAW SCHOOLS

Growth and development in these early schools came haltingly. The common method of preparation for the profession still was through office apprenticeships. Lawyers clung tenaciously to the notion that legal education was nothing more than the mastering of a craft, the skills for which had to be passed on from the practitioner to the novice. And that view was to continue for some time yet to come.

What is more, disruptive political forces of vast proportions were in ferment during the first half of the nineteenth century, which profoundly affected the evolution of legal education and which all but swept away the incipient requirements for bar admission that had been set up in some of the states. It was a period in American history when there occurred a great surge of popular feeling that exalted the rights and powers of the common man. This wave reached its crest with the election of Andrew Jackson, the "apostle of the new democracy," in 1828, but its impact on the attitudes of people as to qualification conditions for public office, requirements of preparation for the professions, and standards on admission to the bar, was to be felt for years to come.[10] Here was a political creed that had no respect for formal education, and particularly one that had no patience with educational prerequisites for the practice of law or the attainment of public office. In its implications this creed seemed to hold that all male citizens had the inherent right to practice law.

[10] Currie, *The Materials of Law Study*, 3 J. Legal Ed. 331, 359–361 (1951); Reed, Present-Day Law Schools in the United States and Canada, 5–9 (Carneg. Found. Bul. 21, 1928).

The effect of this political dogma is difficult to appraise. That it worked a severe setback to the cause of legal education and of standards of bar admission is clear. But that this was only one of a series of consequences also seems clear. In reversing the trend of legal education and of bar admission, this popular doctrine tended to undermine the structure of the legal system. It may be that there was some motivation in this movement to make legal services more accessible to the people, but its effect was to abase the personnel of the legal profession and of the judiciary and to lower the standards of law administration. It was not until toward the end of the century that legal education and the profession began to recover from this reverse.

Thus, university law schools, at the very threshold of their existence, were confronted by a combination of adverse circumstances. A substantial portion of the practicing bar was unconvinced, if not distrustful, of the benefits that might flow to a lawyer through either a university or law-school training. This unbelief and the rising tide of Jacksonian democracy held enrollments in the schools down to a pitiful minimum, and stifled efforts to establish educational requirements for admission to the schools and to the bar.

D. STORY AND THE HARVARD LAW SCHOOL

In the first twelve years of its existence, the Harvard Law School averaged less than nine students a year, and the few who enrolled attended irregularly.[11] That this would result in dissatisfaction over the affairs of the School is evident. In the face of mounting criticism on the part of the Harvard Corporation, Judge Parker resigned in 1827, apparently by request, and Professor Stearns resigned in 1829.[12] The way was now open for a program of

[11] The Centennial History of the Harvard Law School, 5 (1918).
[12] 1 Warren, History of the Harvard Law School, 358, 365 (1908).

reorganization, and the Corporation took decisive action at once to bring about changes in the teaching and administration of the School. The action it took was to be of extreme significance, for, favored by a combination of events, which happily on occasion attend the decisions of men, the measures then adopted by the Corporation injected a vigor into the Harvard Law School which was to start it on its path to a distinguished career as an educational institution. The principal invigorant administered at that time came about through an appointment—through the appointment of Justice Joseph Story as Dane Professor of Law.

In 1829 Nathan Dane, an admirer and disciple of Blackstone, and author of Dane's *General Abridgment and Digest of American Law,* gave a sum of money to Harvard for the establishment of a professorship of law that would bear his name. In making this gift, Dane made the request that Judge Story be appointed the first Dane Professor. He further requested that Story be given time to complete a course of lectures on five branches of the law, and expressed the hope that "all the lectures and teachings of him, and of every professor so to be appointed, shall be calculated to assist and serve in a special manner, law students and lawyers in practice, sound and useful law being the object."[13] Story in accepting the appointment stipulated that another professor be appointed who would assume the responsibilities for the details in the administration of the School. On June 3, 1829, Story was formally elected Dane Professor and a few days later John Hooker Ashmun was appointed to the Royall Professorship. In August following the two new professors were inaugurated. Ashmun's period of service was brief. On his death in 1833, Simon Greenleaf was appointed Royall Professor.

[13] *Ibid,* 420.

Story brought to the Harvard Law School the immense prestige of his name and an infectious enthusiasm for the law. Though he was to continue on the bench for some years yet to come, he was already a great judge, a contemporary of Marshall, with whom he shared the honor of having molded a great supreme court in the formative years of its existence. In the longer view he is one of the towering figures in American judicial history and, along with Marshall and Kent, one of the architects of American law. After graduating from Harvard he studied law in an office. He was one of that brilliant and learned group of lawyers, and pre-eminent among them, of the early post-Revolutionary period. His scholarship was broad and extremely productive. On his appointment at Harvard he had already demonstrated his great ability as a judge, but the time of his most productive scholarship still lay ahead, when in a very short period, from 1832 to 1843, he wrote and published in rapid succession an amazing series of eight treatises on American law. "Of his *Commentaries on the Conflict of Laws* it is not too much to say," observed Warren,[14] "that its publication constituted an epoch in the law; for it became at once the standard and almost the sole authority." Story continued to serve as a justice of the Supreme Court and to teach in the Harvard Law School until his death in 1845.

We pause to wonder and to conjecture why Story accepted the Dane Professorship. It is difficult for us, under the influence of present values, to catch the full significance of his action. Here was a great judge of the Supreme Court accepting a professorship in a school that for the twelve years of its operation had had a mere desultory existence. In the year before Story's arrival, it had had but four

[14] A History of the American Bar, 545 (1911). Pound has made an excellent appraisal of Story in *The Place of Judge Story in the Making of American Law*, 48 Am. L. Rev. 676 (1914).

students. It must have seemed that its life cycle had run. The Dane gift was a factor. Notwithstanding, it is hard to believe that Story's decision was prompted by any immediate attraction. May it be that he envisioned a major contribution to the improvement of legal education? One of his letters gives support to this view. "I have been long persuaded," he wrote to the Principal of the Dublin Law Institute,[15]

> "that a more scientific system of legal education, than that which has hitherto been pursued, is demanded by the wants of the age and the progress of jurisprudence. The old mode of solitary, unassisted studies in the Inns of Court, or in the dry and uninviting drudgery of an office, is utterly inadequate to lay a just foundation for accurate knowledge in the learning of the law. It is for the most part a waste of time and effort, at once discouraging and repulsive. It was, however, the system in which I was myself bred; and so thoroughly convinced was I of its worthlessness, that I then resolved, if ever I had students, I would pursue an opposite course. It was my earnest desire to assist in the establishment of another system, which induced me to accept my present professorship in Harvard University, thereby burthening myself with duties and labors, which otherwise I would gladly have declined."

Story's inaugural address, on the occasion of his installation as Dane Professor, was a major production. He had given much time and thought to its preparation. It was,

[15] Published in 9 Law Reporter, 142 (1846). The Law Reporter also published an interesting extract from a letter written by Professor Greenleaf. He wrote: "In our experience, the advantage of associated or collegiate instruction in the science of law, followed by six to twelve months' attention to the 'manipulations' of practice in a lawyer's office, are beyond all comparison superior to any other method of instruction we have ever known." *Ibid.*

indeed, a disquisition on law and the legal profession, on the study of law and on the objects of the Professorship. There can be no question as to the seriousness with which he viewed his task. Question, if there be any, arises in relation to whether in later performance he fulfilled the high expectation he had engendered through this address. He began by stating[16] that it was his plan to lay before his audience "some considerations touching the general utility of the study of the law," and to "unfold the nature and objects of the professorship." He expressed diffidence on whether he would be able to measure up to the "bright prospects, which the founder" had opened to their view. "In the present state of knowledge," he went on to say,[17]

> "such a diffidence might well become the teacher of any science; but the remark applies with augmented force to a science so vast, so intricate, and so comprehensive, as that of jurisprudence. In its widest extent it may be said almost to compass every human action; and in its minute details, to measure every human duty."

He paid high tribute to Blackstone's *Commentaries* which probably stand, he said, "unrivalled in the literature of any other language," and which are "now studied as a classic in America, as well as in England,"[18] and called attention to the parallel between the Dane gift to Harvard and the earlier Viner gift to Oxford. As did Blackstone in his first lecture for Englishmen, Story recommended[19] "the study of the law to American citizens generally," and expressed his conviction[20] "that a knowledge of the law and a devotion to its principles are vital to a republic, and lie

[16] *Value and Importance of Legal Studies*, in Miscellaneous Writings of Joseph Story, 503 (1852).

[17] *Ibid.*, 504.

[18] *Ibid.*, 547.

[19] *Ibid.*, 511.

[20] *Ibid.*, 512.

at the very foundation of its strength." He then spoke of the duties and responsibilities of the lawyer. "I would exhort the student," he said,[21] "at the very outset of his career, to acquire a just conception of the dignity and importance of his vocation." Upon the "actual administration of justice in all governments," he declared,[22] "and especially in free governments, must depend the welfare of the whole community." The ascent to eminence in the law, he cautioned, is not an easy one; it calls for perseverance, hard work and great ability. "I know not," he observed,[23] "if among human sciences there is any one which requires such various qualifications and extensive attainments as the law." The student must have a thorough knowledge of the principles of the law; but that in itself is not sufficient. He should not imagine, he stressed, "that enough is done, if he has so far mastered the general doctrines of the common law, that he may enter with some confidence into practice. There are other studies, which demand his attention. He should addict himself to the study of philosophy, of rhetoric, of history, and of human nature." It is from a want of this enlarged view of duty, he emphasized, "that the profession has sometimes been reproached with a sordid narrowness, with a low chicane, with a cunning avarice, and with a deficiency in liberal and enlightened policy."[24]

Here was a great judge speaking—a great judge taking just pride in the best in his profession, but not ignoring the worst. Here was one of the most distinguished members of the profession of that or any other time, bearing witness to the qualities that make a lawyer great. "Many of our

[21] *Ibid.*, 518.
[22] *Ibid.*, 519.
[23] *Ibid.*, 522.
[24] *Ibid.*, 527.

most illustrious statesmen have been lawyers," he observed,[25] "but they have been lawyers liberalized by philosophy, and a large intercourse with the wisdom of ancient and modern times. The perfect lawyer, like the perfect orator, must accomplish himself for his duties by familiarity with every study." It is "by such studies, and such accomplishments, that the means are to be prepared for excellence in the highest order of the profession."[26]

A substantial part of his address was devoted to the specific objects of the Professorship. What he had said about the education, the responsibilities, and the qualifications of the lawyer was not to be taken to mean, he remarked, that he believed that the student, after a brief span at Harvard, would forthwith step out a finished product. "Having spoken thus much upon the dignity, the qualifications, and the duties of the profession," he went on to say,[27]

> "I trust it will not be supposed that we have the rashness to indulge the belief that the Law Institutions here, under the guidance of its present Professors, can fill up the outline which has thus been traced . . . Little, indeed, of what has been sketched out in this discourse, can be attained by any academical instruction during the usual period assigned for the preparatory studies for the bar. And of that little, we have not the presumption to believe, that our method or efforts can reach even our own wishes and opinions. What we propose is no more than plain, direct, familiar instruction; something to assist the student in the first steps of his studies; something to cheer him in his progress; something to disencumber him of difficulties by the wayside; and something to awaken a sincere ambition for professional excellence."

[25] *Ibid.*

[26] *Ibid.*, 529.

[27] *Ibid.*, 531–532.

Under the distinguished leadership of Story, and the efficient administration of the School by Ashmun, and later by Greenleaf, enrollments increased. In the first year after the advent of Story it had 24; in 1839 it had 86; by 1841 it had 115; and in 1844, the year before Story's death, the number had mounted to 163.[28] What Story did for the advancement of legal education is, however, a subject for debate. That he did not substantially liberalize the course of instruction is clear. Liberal studies, if taken at all while the student was preparing for the bar, had to be pursued before he began his law studies. This was in accord with the views Story had expressed in his inaugural address. In referring to one of his assignments as Dane Professor, that dealing with the law of nature, he said that this "involves a consideration of the nature, faculties, and responsibilities of man." It involves dealing with man "in the various relations of life, in which he may be placed, . . . as a solitary being, as a member of a family, as a parent, and lastly, as a member of the commonwealth."[29] As he viewed it, the subject touched, among other things, "the nature and limits of social liberty; the structure of civil and political rights; the authority and policy of laws; and, indeed, all those institutions which form the defence and the ornament of civilized society."[30] He then went on to say that on many of these topics he would speak but briefly and with reserve, and this for two reasons: "In the first place, in the course of the academical instruction in this University already provided for, the subjects of ethics, natural law, and theology, are assigned to other professors. In the next place, in the elementary education, everywhere

---

[28] Reed, Training for the Public Profession of the Law, 143 (Carneg. Found. Bul. 15, 1921).

[29] Supra, note 16, p. 535.

[30] *Ibid.*

passed through before entering upon juridical studies, they are usually taught with sufficient fulness and accuracy."[31]

This raises the oft-recurring question as to what should be taught in a law school and what should be assumed to have been taught adequately by other educational agencies. Story's statement, however, reveals an hiatus. His law school did not demand any preliminary education; it did not even require its students "to have enough education to be admitted to college."[32] While many who entered the School had had college work, it was not a *sine qua non* for all students. How then could Story say that they had had sufficient instruction in the fields under discussion? What seems to be clear is that under Story, whether he so viewed it or not, a momentous step in the development of legal education was taken. Leaders before him, including Blackstone, Jefferson, Kent, and Hoffman, had conceived of the study of law as a part of a liberal education. Under Story liberal and legal instruction were divorced, and as to liberal education all that remained was the assumption that students had somehow gotten it elsewhere. "In more respects than one," observed Professor Currie,[33]

> "the character of university legal education in America for generations to come was shaped by these events. The immediate practical success of the educational enterprise which Story conducted on this strictly professional basis is unchallengeable; so also is the dignity with which he clothed that enterprise by the remarkable productivity of his scholarship. . . . The traditional attitudes of American law schools toward local law, legislation, and criminal law can all be traced

[31] *Ibid.*, 536. Story also touches on this subject in another address, *The Science of Government*, in Miscellaneous Writings, 614, 629 (1852).

[32] Reed, supra, note 28, p. 145.

[33] *The Materials of Law Study*, 3 J. Legal Ed. 331, 366 (1951).

to decisions made in the course of Story's reorganization. . . . not even Langdell's case method, the best known of all Harvard influences, has had a more pervasive and significant effect on legal education than was produced by the steps taken during Story's administration to define the part to be played by non-technical studies in the education of the lawyer. With respect to the place of such studies in the law school itself, Story's judgment was not seriously challenged until the 1920's, when the modern movement toward integration of law with other social studies began."

This is an accurate appraisal of the impact of the Story period on legal education. What Story accomplished or failed to accomplish should, however, be appraised in the context of the time in which he worked. Then university law schools were in their swaddling clothes. The approved method of preparation for the bar was through office apprenticeships, and members of the bar generally were skeptical of the values accruing to a lawyer from either a liberal or a law-school education. Bar admission requirements, the barometer for standards of legal education, were low or non-existent. There were indeed a few men, of whom Story was one, who had an enlightened conception of the significance of law to a free society and of the need for its formulation and administration by a liberally educated bar, but their utterances were of little or no avail against the insistent voices of the rising Jacksonian democracy.

The severely legal content of the course of instruction established during the Story period is, it is true, open to criticism, and particularly so in the light of the views Story had expressed in his inaugural address. But Story did put on its feet a faltering law school and did give to that school an impetus that was to carry it later to distinction. He did more than that, and this is extremely important:

Through the extraordinary productiveness of his scholarship, he set a magnificent example for all future generations of law teachers. Our criticism perhaps should be directed against those who followed Story for their tardiness, when circumstances were more favorable for the schools, in broadening the foundations he had laid. It was not until the 1870's that the schools made moves toward the establishment of liberal education prerequisites for admission to law study; it was not until the forepart of the present century that there occurred any clear development aimed to bring about an integration of law and the social studies; it was not until after World War II that the schools began to wonder whether their course of instruction was geared to train the student in the essential skills of the profession; and it was not until then that they made any serious effort to integrate theory and practical instruction into a comprehensive program of legal education.

V. THE CASE METHOD

A. Law Schools, 1839–1870

In the years following the reorganization of the Harvard Law School under Story, the number of schools gradually increased. By 1850 there were fifteen; by 1860 the number was twenty-one; and by 1870 it was thirty-one. Even as late as 1870 a substantial number of the schools, twelve of the thirty-one, conducted one-year programs; two had lengthened the course to one and a half years; and seventeen were on a two-year basis. The instruction offered was severely legal. A number of states had by 1870 established a requirement that all applicants for admission to the bar had to be twenty-one years of age. The schools had no entrance qualifications, except an occasional recognition of the maturity standard; for example, Harvard after 1849 had a requirement that an applicant for law study must be a person of good moral character and nineteen years of age.[1]

Instruction was by lectures supplemented by text assignments. The course in the Harvard Law School for the year 1855–1856 is typical. Parker lectured on bailments, constitutional law and the jurisprudence of the United States, equity jurisprudence, pleading, evidence, and practice; Parsons gave lectures on Blackstone, insurance, bills and notes, and partnership; Washburn lectured on domestic relations, conflict of laws, sales and real property.[2] In appraising the Harvard Law School as it was immediately before the advent of Langdell, Ames spoke of it as "a school without examination for admission or for the degree."

[1] Reed, Training for the Public Profession of the Law, 171, 315 (Carneg. Found. Bul. 15, 1921).

[2] 2 Warren, History of the Harvard Law School, 218 (1908).

It had, said he, "a faculty of three professors giving but ten lectures a week to one hundred and fifteen students of whom fifty-three per cent had no college degree, a curriculum without any rational sequence of subjects, and an inadequate and decaying library."[3] This, we should observe, is a description of what had come to be regarded as the foremost law school in America. Seemingly the school had made little or no advance since the days of Story. On its staff, indeed, it did not have the equivalent of a Story.

Measured by perceptible standards, progress in legal education in America up to 1870 is disappointing. Through the years lawyers had come to the bar through the desultory method of private reading and office apprenticeships; that in 1870 was still the common route to the profession. The highlights of the preceding century were the career of the Litchfield School; the establishment of the university law professorships; the creation of a law school at Harvard, followed by the organization of other university law schools; the rebirth of the Harvard Law School under Story. What is significant is that the foundations had been laid. The great pioneers in legal education had had to contend with the apathy of a profession absorbed in the routine tasks of a craft, and the enervating popular philosophy of Jacksonian democracy. The sparks of the fire kindled by those pioneers, however, remained, ready to be fanned into a blaze. By 1870 changes in legal education were in order. "Events now demanded of the bar knowledge and skills not within the sonorous phrases of the 'constitutional lawyer' of mid-century or the black-letter learning of the conveyancer."[4] It is unfortunate that the men who were to shape the policies of legal education in the truly remarkable era that lay ahead, when the fires again were burning, projected

[3] *Christopher Columbus Langdell,* in Lectures on Legal History, 467, 477 (1913).

[4] Hurst, The Growth of American Law, 260 (1950).

their programs on a narrow conception of the functions of law and that they laid so heavy a stress on method.

Much of the discussion touching the case system of instruction is concerned with method. We must not underrate the importance of method. Method is of particular significance in scientific research where its main function is to provide a rational and systematic procedure and so eliminate error so far as possible in the field under investigation. Educational method involves a plan for presenting the materials of instruction. Educational method, however, must never be looked upon as anything more than an instrument of teaching. The one essential of effective education is the great teacher, regardless of method. The lecture method has limitations but many highly stimulating teachers have made their contributions to the learning of their pupils through lectures. One of the greatest teachers of all time made no text assignments, delivered no lectures, and wrote nothing. Socrates asked questions, and through that approach to teaching became the exponent of a method that bears his name. "Yet methods, particularly successful methods, are often more powerful than beliefs. The overwhelming success of the case method tended to crystallize and to carry into a later period a conception of the proper scope of legal study that was dominant when this method was receiving its first mold. If the case method could have originated in 1810 and have received its initial impress from the thinking of that period, it is a safe assumption that legal education would today have a much broader scope that it actually has."[5]

B. THE INFLUENCE OF LANGDELL

The credit for originating the case method of law instruction is generally and properly given to Christopher Colum-

[5] Preliminary Statement of the Committee on Legal Education of the Harvard Law School, 95 (1947).

bus Langdell. Baldwin has pointed out that Judge Zephaniah Swift of Connecticut published the first casebook in the United States in 1810. Judge Swift prepared for the use of students who studied in his office a short treatise on evidence, of 174 pages, "with an appendix, containing the principal cases to which reference was made in it, covering 68 pages." Judge Baldwin also has mentioned that even before Langdell at least one American law school followed the practice of assigning cases to its students for collateral reading.[6] Elihu Root between 1865 and 1867 studied cases in New York University under John Norton Pomeroy. Pomeroy's method, said Jessup,[7] "was not unlike the case system later perfected by Langdell. The students were expected to read cases and then to be questioned on them in class." But case study and case instruction as an exclusive, all-absorbing educational method came in with Langdell. It was originated by Langdell and was defined and made a fighting faith by his early disciples. It is the prevailing method of legal education today, with this difference: where once the conception of it had a singleness and fidelity of purpose, it now has taken on chameleon characteristics. The situation presents a seeming contradiction. Law schools today follow the "case method" of instruction. The modern casebook in content and scope shows a wide departure from the premises established for this method by Langdell. The schools still give apparent obeisance to Langdell's conception. Clearly the case system of instruction, since its initiation by Langdell, has undergone great changes. It remains to be seen how far this departure from Langdell and the other founders has also worked a transition toward broadening the scope of legal education. But before entering into a discussion of the

[6] *Education for the Bar in the United States,* 4 Am. Law School Rev. 8, 13 (1915).

[7] 1 Elihu Root, 61 (1938).

wider implications of this transition, we shall first want to be clear on how the founders viewed this subject.

Langdell became Dane Professor of Law in the Harvard Law School in January 1870. In September of that year he was appointed to the newly created office of dean of the Law School. He held that position for twenty-five years. He had attended the Harvard Law School from 1851 to 1854. From 1854 to 1870 he was in the practice of law in New York City. There he had the reputation, with the few individuals who knew him, of being well-read in the law and of being extremely studious. His work was almost entirely restricted to office practice. When appointed at Harvard he was very nearly unknown in the profession.[8] Yet this was the man whom President Eliot appointed Dane Professor and forthwith dean of the School. The contrast between his appointment and that of Story is striking. Sixteen years later Eliot explained his action. "I remembered," said he,[9]

> "that when I was a Junior in College in the year 1851–1852, and used to go often in the early evening to the room of a friend who was in the Divinity School, I there heard a young man who was making notes to *Parsons on Contracts* talk about law. He was generally eating his supper at the time, standing up in front of the fire and eating with good appetite a bowl of brown bread and milk. I was a mere boy, only eighteen years old; but it was given to me to understand that I was listening to a man of genius. In the year 1870, I recalled the remarkable character of that young man's

[8] Ames, *Christopher Columbus Langdell*, in Lectures on Legal History, 467, 471–472 (1913); 2 Warren, History of the Harvard Law School, 359–360 (1908).

[9] Quoted by Warren, *ibid.*, 360–361; also quoted in part by Ames, *ibid.*, 473.

> expositions, sought him in New York, and induced him to become Dane Professor. So he became Professor Langdell. He then told me, in 1870, a great many of the things he has told you this afternoon: I have heard most of his speech before. He told me that law was a science: I was quite prepared to believe it. He told me that the way to study a science was to go to the original sources. I knew that was true, for I had been brought up in the science of chemistry myself; and one of the first rules of a conscientious student of science is never to take a fact or a principle out of second hand treatises, but to go to the original memoir of the discoverer of that fact or principle."

Langdell published his first casebook, *A Selection of Cases on the Law of Contracts,* in 1871. No fanfare accompanied its appearance. Langdell was ever unassuming. In fact, even when his method was under severest attack, he said very little in its defense, and apparently nothing in direct reply to criticism. Characteristically, the preface to his casebook was brief. "I entered upon the duties of my present position, a year and a half ago," he commented,[10] "with a settled conviction that law could only be taught or learned effectively by means of cases in some form." But how was this scheme to be put into effect? Here he encountered what first seemed to him to be "an insuperable practical difficulty, namely, the want of books."[11] He could not set a whole class to work reading cases in the library. The solution to the problem appeared to be that he publish a selection of cases. But how was this to be done? In view of the great number of reported cases, "was there any satisfactory principle upon which such a selection could be

---

[10] A Selection of Cases on the Law of Contracts, Preface, vii (1871).

[11] *Ibid.*, viii.

made?"[12] He believed there was. "Law, considered as a science,"[13] said he,

> "consists of certain principles or doctrines. To have such a mastery of these as to be able to apply them with constant facility and certainty to the ever-tangled skein of human affairs, is what constitutes a true lawyer; and hence to acquire that mastery should be the business of every earnest student of law. Each of these doctrines has arrived at its present state by slow degrees; in other words, it is a growth, extending in many cases through centuries. This growth is to be traced in the main through a series of cases; and much the shortest and best, if not the only way of mastering the doctrine effectually is by studying the cases in which it is embodied. But the cases which are useful and necessary for this purpose at the present day bear an exceedingly small proportion to all that have been reported. The vast majority are useless, and worse than useless, for any purpose of systematic study. Moreover, the number of fundamental legal doctrines is much less than is commonly supposed; the many different guises in which the same doctrine is constantly making its appearance, and the great extent to which legal treatises are a repetition of each other, being a cause of much misapprehension. If these doctrines could be so classified and arranged that each should be found in its proper place, and nowhere else, they would cease to be formidable from their number."

In these brief words Langdell stated his basic assumptions. Law is a science, and as such it consists of certain principles or doctrines. These doctrines, relatively few in

[12] *Ibid.*
[13] *Ibid.*, viii–ix.

number, are to be found in the decisions of the courts, the sources of the common law. A true lawyer must have mastered these doctrines, and he must have the ability to apply them in the solution of the complicated problems of human relations. Of the great mass of cases only a selected number merit consideration for study; the rest are useless. Through carefully selected cases, classified and arranged, the essential doctrines of the law—in their evolution and present validity—can be taught and learned. This, indeed, so Langdell believed, is the only effective way law can be taught or learned.

Fifteen years later he stated what he considered to be the underlying reasons for teaching and learning law in a university.[14] He started from the premises: "First, that law is a science; *secondly, that all the available materials of that science are contained in printed books* [emphasis added]. If law be not a science," he reasoned,

> "a university will best consult its own dignity in declining to teach it. If it be not a science, it is a species of handicraft, and may best be learned by serving an apprenticeship to one who practices it. If it be a science, it will scarcely be disputed that it is one of the greatest and most difficult of sciences, and that it needs all the light that the most enlightened seat of learning can throw upon it. Again, law can be learned and taught in a university by means of printed books. If, therefore, there are other and better means of teaching and learning law than printed books, or if printed books can only be used to the best advantage in connection with other means,—for instance, the work of a lawyer's office, or attendance upon the pro-

[14] From an address before the Harvard Law School Association, 1886. Quoted, 2 Warren, History of the Harvard Law School, 374 (1908).

> ceedings of courts of justice,—it must be confessed that such means cannot be provided by a university. But if printed books are the ultimate sources of all legal knowledge; if every student who would obtain any mastery of law as a science must resort to these ultimate sources; and if the only assistance which it is possible for the learner to receive is such as can be afforded by teachers who have travelled the same road before him,—then a university, and a university alone, can furnish every possible facility for teaching and learning law."

We are dealing here with the most significant event in the evolution of American legal education and it poses a situation that is paradoxical. Langdell introduced, and his early disciples perfected, a system of instruction which in the hands of an able and skillful teacher is unexcelled as an instrument of education. What is more, Langdell and his followers definitely and firmly implanted the teaching of law in the universities. Blackstone and others had pointed the way and had spoken persuasively on this subject, but when Langdell appeared, the time was right for the consummation of this movement. But Langdell also is responsible more than any other man for confining legal education in a strait mold which was for years to dissociate it from the living context of the world about it. The dictum was that all the available materials of the law were contained in printed books, and the printed books from which and only from which a legal education was to be had were casebooks consisting of selected decisions of the appellate courts on each of the main topics of the law. Disregarded were the broad premises for the study of law conceived by those men who held the initial professorships of law. Unrecognized was the fact that prospective lawyers needed training in various areas of learning and skill. "The prevailing view came to be that law is and can be self-sufficient, that its premises are essentially legal in nature, that the process of deducing conclusions from these premises involves no recourse to anything beyond the law itself and its own internal history. Toward the end of the nineteenth century this view came to be almost an article of faith with lawyers, not only in this country but in England and Europe as well."[15]

C. EARLY DISCIPLES OF LANGDELL

The merits of the case system were better described by Langdell's disciples, and particularly by Ames and Keener, than by Langdell himself, and in their portrayals we find also the first evidences of some shift in emphasis from Langdell's position. James Barr Ames is one of the great figures in American legal education. "The forty years of his connection with the Harvard Law School was its golden age: the period which President Eliot and Langdell inaugurated but no one did more than Ames to crown with success. He was a member of Langdell's first class and his devoted disciple; and he even more than Langdell himself established the so-called 'Langdell method' of studying and teaching law."[16] Ames was more flexible in his thinking and outlook on the subject of teaching law than Langdell and perhaps more discerning. "Different methods," he observed,[17]

> "have prevailed at different times and places. At the Litchfield School, Judge Reeve and Judge Gould divided the law into forty-eight titles and prepared written lectures on these titles which they delivered, or rather

[15] Preliminary Statement of the Committee on Legal Education of the Harvard Law School, 94–95 (1947).

[16] *Memior of James Barr Ames* in Ames, Lectures on Legal History, 3, 8 (1913).

[17] Ames, *The Vocation of the Law Professor,* in Lectures on Legal History, 354, 362 (1913).

> dictated to the students, who took as accurate notes as possible, which they afterwards filled out and copied for preservation. . . . At a time when there were very few legal treatises, this plan of supplying the students with manuscript text-books served a useful purpose."

There was no doubt, however, in Ames' mind as to the superiority of the case system. "The object arrived at by us at Cambridge," he stressed,[18] "is the power of legal reasoning, and we think we can best get that by putting before the students the best models to be found in the history of English and American law." If it be, said he,[19]

> "the professor's object that his students shall be able to discriminate between the relevant and the irrelevant facts of a case, to draw just distinctions between things apparently similar, and to discover true analogies between things apparently dissimilar, in a word, that they shall be sound legal thinkers, competent to grapple with new problems because of their experience in mastering old ones, I know of no better course for him to pursue than to travel with his class through a wisely chosen collection of cases."

Writing in 1888, Professor Keener, in the preface to his casebook, *A Selection of Cases on the Law of Quasi-Contracts*, observed that the method of teaching by cases had, since its introduction, steadily grown in favor. "While this method of teaching," he commented,[20]

---

[18] 31 Rep. Am. Bar Ass'n, 1025 (1907).

[19] *The Vocation of the Law Professor*, in Lectures on Legal History, 354, 364 (1913).

[20] Vol. I, pp. v–vi. Keener later expanded his views in an address: *The Inductive Method in Legal Education*, 17 Rep. Am. Bar Ass'n, 473 (1894). Among those who appeared on the program with Keener on that occasion were: Henry Wade Rogers, John F. Dillon, John D. Lawson, Simeon E. Baldwin, Woodrow Wilson, and John H. Wigmore.

"does not at all proceed on the idea that the common law is wanting in jurists, its advocates regard the adjudged cases as the original sources of our law, and think that it is better for the student, under proper advice and guidance, to extract from the cases a principle, than to accept the statement of any jurist, however eminent he may be, that a certain principle is established by certain cases. When the student has by the study of cases grasped a principle, it has assumed to him a concrete form, and he can apply it because it was by studying it in its application that he has acquired his knowledge. Under this system the student must look upon law as a science consisting of a body of principles to be found in the adjudged cases, the cases being to him what the specimen is to the geologist . . . By this method the student's reasoning powers are constantly developed, and while he is gaining the power of legal analysis and synthesis, he is also gaining the other object of legal education, namely, a knowledge of what the law actually is."

D. LATER APPRAISAL OF THE CASE METHOD

It must not be taken that there is or has ever been a single method of case teaching. The common denominator is that the instructors use, as a common basis of instruction, in each of the separate courses, a selection of cases. Every teacher, said Thayer,[21] "in law, as in other things, has his own methods, determined by his own gifts or lack of gifts,—methods as incommunicable as his temperament, his looks, or his manners." Professor Lon Fuller in a brief sentence, in his report to the Survey of the Legal Profession on legal education in Pennsylvania, well described case instruction as "a method which involves a joint exploration

[21] 1 Cases on Constitutional Law, vi (1895).

of problems by instructor and class as contrasted with a method designed primarily to convey information from the instructor to the class."[22] From this premise, he found, "taking the Pennsylvania schools as a whole, good case method instruction is a rarity. In this," he went on to say, "I do not think they are different from other law schools, including our most famous, for I am convinced that there is a decline in the use of the case method over the country as a whole."[23] Professor Fuller's observations led him to believe that case instruction has been virtually supplanted by lectures or quizzes.

Professor Edmund M. Morgan in a careful analysis of the case method as it is employed in the schools today spoke of it has having "all shades of value." He classified three principal varieties,[24] one, in which the instructor uses the reported case "merely as a vehicle for imparting information concerning legal doctrine." He found nothing to commend in this approach. Through it the student gets no more than a passing acquaintance with legal doctrines and even as to them he will cover less ground in a given period of time with cases than through text reading and lectures. In the second variety the instructor goes a step further: "he insists on a careful statement of the facts, requiring the student to discard details of no legal significance and to include all those having a material bearing upon the legal relations of the parties." Under this method the instructor requires the student to have a thorough understanding of the case and nothing more. There are educational values in this method but it falls substantially short of the best practices of case instruction. The majority of teachers, Professor Morgan believed, do much more.

[22] *Legal Education and Admissions to the Bar in Pennsylvania,* 25 Temp. L. Q. 249, 263 (1952).

[23] *Ibid.*

[24] *The Case Method,* 4 J. Legal Ed. 379, 383–384 (1952).

They are the artists of his third classification. And here we observe that Morgan made a more favorable appraisal of present-day case teaching than did Professor Fuller. The third variety involves the best educational uses of the case method. The instructor in this category "varies the manner of handling the cases. He may begin with a statement of a case by the student, or by putting a hypothetical state of facts varying only in immaterial details from the case in the text." As the discussion proceeds he may submit divergent fact situations. He encourages the student to think, to discriminate, to make an evaluation on the fairness of the decision, and to arrive at his own conclusions about the case. At the end the instructor may inform the student on the results reached by other courts on the issue under discussion and as to whether the doctrines evolved have been modified by statute. This, it would appear, is what Ames meant by the instructor's traveling "with his class through a wisely chosen collection of cases;" what Keener meant by developing the student's reasoning powers, and his powers of analysis and synthesis; and what Fuller meant by "a joint exploration of problems by instructor and class."[25]

E. DEVELOPMENTS IN THE CASE METHOD

The case method of instruction is difficult to define for still another reason: the variable properties of the materials included in the several casebooks. Clearly, the casebook has gone through a process of evolution in content and scope since Langdell's work on contracts, but the diversified

[25] In a recent article Professor Patterson presents an excellent appraisal of the case method from a somewhat different approach: *The Case Method in American Legal Education: Its Origins and Objectives*, 4 J. Legal Ed. 1 (1951). He has made a valuable contribution in his appraisal of the fourfold presuppositions of the case method, namely, scientific, pedagogical, pragmatic, and historical.

current crop of casebooks cannot be classified wholly as the end-product of evolution. Beyond general points of similarity among casebooks, there is today no common pattern. As methods of case teaching, to use Thayer's words, are determined by the instructor's "own gifts or lack of gifts," so likewise the modern casebook is determined by the gifts of its editor, by the notions he has about legal education, and, on occasion, by his idiosyncrasies.[26]

Langdell believed that a casebook should contain a selection of leading or influential cases, and apparently nothing more. His view was that the number of basic doctrines of the law was limited, and that it was feasible to select, classify, and arrange all the cases on a subject, for example, contracts, "which had contributed in any important degree to the growth, development, or establishment of any of its essential doctrines."[27] The criterion of selection was: had the case substantially contributed to the development of the essential doctrines of the law? The cases that passed that test were then arranged in chronological sequence under conceptual headings. Langdell's cases were unedited and were almost devoid of note citations. Ames initiated the first major departure in appending copious annotations to his cases.

Wherein do the modern casebooks differ from their prototypes? To answer this question is to risk trying to do what is well-nigh impossible, for, as we have observed, there is today no typical casebook. There are, however, some major trends that can be described. Generally, current casebooks lay less stress than the earlier ones on historical

---

[26] "In these days, when so-called case-books range from the bizarre to the prosaic, from mere reprints of reported decisions and citations of other opinions to heterogeneous collections of diverse materials, one may question whether there is such a thing as a typical case-book." Wilson (Book Review), 25 Corn. L. Q. 653, 655 (1940).

[27] A Selection of Cases on the Law of Contracts, *Preface*, ix (1871).

development. Langdell's concept of influential cases presupposed a selection of cases that had left their mark on the growth of the law. This meant selecting old cases from economic or social contexts which were strange to the student. The modern casebook is pragmatic and stresses recent cases. The tendency is to select cases that deal with what Professor Patterson has called the "contemporary culture" in which the student "lives and in which legal devices are operative."[28] Controversies touching facts in the student's environmental ken—for example, buying and selling radios and automobiles, installment buying, etc.—are thought to claim his interest to a higher degree than those dealing with legal settings with which he is not familiar. "What slows up case-instruction," observed Llewellyn,[29] "is the student's lack of grasp of the background of life and meaning. When will we wake up to what we all know? Strange facts mean slow reading."

In the older books cases were grouped under conceptual titles; the conceptual classification still is retained, but in recent years a number of casebook editors have experimented with a functional approach. The basic concepts have an amazing tenacity. "One very good reason for this is that despite twenty-five years or more of washing legal concepts in the cynical acid of legal realism American courts continue to employ many surviving and pervasive concepts in their opinions."[30] We must not take it, however, that the established order is withstanding attack unscathed. In a stimulating and provocative article Lasswell and McDougal have proposed that the materials of law study should be re-

---

[28] *The Case Method in American Legal Education: Its Origins and Objectives*, 4 J. Legal Ed. 1, 15 (1951).

[29] *On the Problem of Teaching "Private" Law*, 54 Harv. L. Rev. 775, 792 (1941).

[30] Patterson, supra, note 28, p. 15.

organized to stress the policy needs of society.[31] They accept "the traditional assumption that it is imperative for the student to acquaint himself with the established legal syntax,"[32] but argue for a new outlook and approach. "A first indispensable step toward the effective reform of legal education," they contend, "is to clarify ultimate aim. We submit," said they,[33] "this basic proposition: if legal education in the contemporary world is adequately to serve the needs of a free and productive commonwealth, it must be conscious, efficient, and systematic *training for policy-making.*" It is obvious, they believe, "that our existing law school curriculum is not adequately oriented toward achieving the distinctive values and conditioning variables of a free society."[34] The major purpose of legal education, they maintain,[35] "is to promote the adaptation of legal education to the policy needs of a free society." The authors deserve high credit for their emphasis on the need for raising the sights of legal education from the routine of case study to more important objectives, but they have over-simplified the problem in stressing policy-making as *the* aim in legal education.[36]

Two more trends relative to the makeup and content of casebooks should be mentioned, namely, the editing of the cases—the chopping out of unessential statements—and the insertion, in some of the books, of text and extra-legal materials. Excepting only the headnotes, Langdell printed whole cases, including the arguments of counsel. Today, to make

---

[31] *Legal Education and Public Policy: Professional Training in the Public Interest*, 52 Yale L. J. 203 (1943).

[32] *Ibid.*, 243.

[33] *Ibid.*, 206.

[34] *Ibid.*, 232.

[35] *Ibid.*, 243.

[36] Llewellyn has discussed Lasswell and McDougal's article in, *McDougal and Lasswell Plan for Legal Education*, 43 Colum. L. Rev. 476 (1943).

room for a widening variety of case law, legislation and other materials, the cases are being severely edited and statements of fact in the cases often are being shortened by restatements of them. The reasons for these moves are various. The most obvious is to cover more ground and so to include the expanding law. The pressure to give more than passing attention to and to supply information on the growing law is a very real one and is creating well-nigh unsolvable curricular problems. The individual who has the job of wrestling with these problems must often have the unhappy experience, as did Hercules in combat with Antaeus, just when he is confident he has brought them down to Mother Earth, of having them spring up again with renewed vigor. The scope of the law in the human interests and institutions it touches is constantly increasing, principally today through the introduction of vast new fields of legislation and administrative regulations. The older subjects have been expanded, and new ones, for example, taxation, administrative law, and labor law, unthought-of in Langdell's time, have been added. All this tends to depreciate the older values of case teaching and to substitute in their place emphasis on informational content. "Case-instruction is today threatened with slow suffocation under a constant accession of new and more complex materials and new and more complex demands which are made upon all case-courses at once and indiscriminately, and of which materials and demands only a severely limited number can be handled effectively and down through a whole class in the time allotted to any particular case-course."[37]

This trend to include non-case materials in the casebooks has today become a common practice. Cases are being interspersed with text discussions, excerpts from law review

[37] *Report of Committee on Curriculum,* Handbook, Ass'n Am. L. Schools, 159, 170 (1944).

articles, reproductions of statutes, legal forms and various other materials. The reasons for these moves are almost as diverse as the personalities of the respective individuals who compile these works.[38] Packing more information into the books is a prominent one. Closely related is the attempt, a belated move to be sure, to give recognition to the fact that the context of law is complex and that it consists of more than mere judge-made law. The insertion of legal forms in the books probably arises from awareness on the part of teachers that students should be familiarized with the basic skills of the practicing lawyer.

Another substantial reason for this development relates to the objective of broadening the scope of the student's education. To that end a substantial amount of extra-legal material is being inserted into the modern casebook. It may be questionable whether that is a good way, as an educational device, to open the windows of the student's mind to these areas of learning. Be that as it may, the inclusion of extra-legal materials in the casebooks represents a trend in legal education that during the last two or three decades has become ever more apparent. The literal case-law instructor is today a rarity. A new generation of teachers is taking over. The new teacher believes that case instruction is a vital factor in legal education, but he recognizes also that law does not operate in a vacuum; that it must not be isolated from the world about it; that other disciplines are intimately related to law; and that the materials of law study and law instruction must be broadened to give the legal neophyte insight into the interplay of the complex forces that create the need for law and that must be taken into account in its administration. This, in essence, is a return to the views held on legal education by those brilliant

[38] Ehrenzweig has a good analysis of the evolution of the casebook in *The American Casebook: "Cases and Materials,"* 32 Geo. L.J. 224 (1944).

lawyer-teachers of the post-Revolutionary period. There is, however, this difference: Whereas those able men spoke and labored at a time when the profession and the public were not prepared mentally and materially to put these programs into effect, the time is now ripe for their initiation. The scope of this development must not, however, be overstated, for it still is in its incipient stages and its substance and direction are yet uncertain. Later I shall wish to return to this subject in relation to our examination of the principal criticisms of modern legal education.

VI. IMPACT OF PROFESSIONAL ORGANIZATIONS

A. Import of the Profession

A perspective on legal education discloses that while its progress is affected by many agencies, those to the actions of which it is most sensitive are the profession itself and the instrumentalities for bar admission. They are all, indeed, parts of a common machinery. The status of each is affected by movements and changes in the others. It was impossible for legal education to have a wholesome development so long as the profession was apathetic to it and the standards of bar admission were low; but whether apathetic or active, the attitude of the profession is reflected in the progress of legal education. The profession has always, with the possible exception of the Colonial period, had some able individuals who spoke with clarity and with surprising unanimity of view on the subject of legal education. These men left their imprint on it. But they spoke only for themselves and not as representatives of the bar, which too often was passive if not hostile to their views. Legal education could not flourish in this climate. It was not until the bar became organized and its leaders were able to express the views of the organized bar that the profession as such became a dynamic and guiding force, instead of an impediment, in this area.

Bar associations of a sort had existed for some time before 1878, when the American Bar Association was founded. Their functions were mainly social. Occasionally they were established for special purposes, for example, the maintenance of libraries. Legal education and standards of admission to the bar were given some, but desultory attention by these early associations. After the Civil War a new generation of lawyers, stimulated into action by the prevalence of corruption in politics and government in which lawyers and judges were involved, assumed leadership and began pressing for measures of reform. Among their objectives was improvement in legal education. By the 1870's a strong movement was under way in the profession to establish bar associations. During that decade at least eight city and eight state associations were founded. That decade saw also the advent of the American Bar Association. We are stressing primarily, in this study, the impact and influence on the development of legal education of two professional organizations—the American Bar Association and the Association of American Law Schools. This must, however, not be taken as an indication that the work of state and local associations has been insignificant in this field. The value of their contributions has been dependent on instant leadership and has been variable; but this observation holds for the work of all organizations. At times they have given excellent guidance and support to the programs of legal education; at other times they have been unconcerned. In the main, they have followed the lead of the American Bar Association, serving as vehicles through which that Association has carried out its programs.[1]

B. THE ABA—ITS ORGANIZATION AND IMMEDIATE INTEREST IN LEGAL EDUCATION

The call for a meeting "to form an American Bar Association," dated July 1, 1878, was signed by a group of dis-

[1] The story of the contributions to legal education by the American Bar Association and the Association of American Law Schools has been told in an excellent report to the Survey of the Legal Profession by Professor R. N. Sullivan, *Professional Associations and Legal Education,* 4 J. Legal Ed. 401 (1952). It is to be noted that Professor Sullivan was the acting adviser to the American Bar Association's Section of Legal Education and Admissions to the Bar during the fateful years of World War II.

tinguished lawyers. The dominant figure in the movement was Judge Simeon E. Baldwin—lawyer, judge, statesman, and legal educator. Judge Baldwin is a man of impressive stature in the history of the legal profession. To him goes the credit of being the father of the American Bar Association.

At the organizational meeting, held in August 1878 at Saratoga, New York, Carleton Hunt of Louisiana reported for the "Committee on Framing a Constitution," and submitted a draft of the Constitution. This report with some slight amendments was approved and the Constitution was adopted. Among the standing committees of the Association named in this Constitution was that *On Legal Education and Admissions to the Bar*.[2] In the proceedings of this, the first meeting of the American Bar Association, there also is recorded the following motion which was approved:[3]

> "Mr. Hunt offered the following resolution: That the Committee on Legal Education and Admissions to the Bar be instructed to report, at the ensuing annual meeting, some plan for assimilating throughout the Union, the requirements of candidates for admission to the bar, and for regulating, on principles of comity, the standing, throughout the Union, of gentlemen already admitted to practice in their own States."

Later, when the committees for 1878–1879 were appointed, Mr. Hunt was named chairman of the newly created "Committee on Legal Education and Admissions to the Bar." Thus it appears that legal education and bar admissions were subjects of concern to the American Bar Association from the time of its origin, and that Carleton Hunt is one of the unsung heroes in the drama of legal education.[4]

---

[2] 1 Rep. Am. Bar Ass'n, 16 (1878).

[3] *Ibid.*, 26.

[4] Carleton Hunt of New Orleans was "the son of the president of

When the Association met for its second annual meeting in 1879, Mr. Hunt reported for his committee. His supporting statement was a learned dissertation on legal education. He stressed the importance of law-school training. "There is little if any dispute now," he said,[5] "as to the relative merit of education by means of law schools, and that to be got by mere practical training or apprenticeship as an attorney's clerk. Without disparagement of mere practical advantages, the verdict of the best informed is in favor of the schools." He observed, however, while some schools were doing commendable work, there were others which were not deserving of approval. After making his statement, he presented the recommendations of the committee, which consisted of four resolutions. The first re-emphasized the resolution relative to the establishment of principles of comity to govern admission to the bar in the several states that Hunt had presented to the Association the year before. In the second resolution the committee recommended that state and local bar associations be urged to further, in their respective states, "the maintenance by public authority, of schools of law, *provided with faculties of at least four well paid and efficient teachers*" [emphasis added]. It is to be observed that the proposal for a minimum of four teachers for each school was a goal that only recently has been attained. It should be added that the goal, in the form of a requirement, that they be *well paid* has not yet been attained.

The third and fourth resolutions of the committee merit special attention. They were:[6]

---

the University of Louisiana, a graduate of Harvard College, and of the law school which later became Tulane and of which he was then Dean." Seavey, *The Association of American Law Schools in Retrospect*, 3 J. Legal Ed. 153, 155 (1950).

[5] 2 Rep. Am. Bar Ass'n, 209, 216 (1879).

[6] *Ibid.*, 14–15, 235–236.

> "*Resolved,* That the said state and other local bar associations be respectfully requested to recommend and further in such law schools a general course of instruction, to be duly divided, for ordinary purposes, into studies and exercises of the first year, of the second year, and of the third year, including at least the following studies:" Moral and Political Philosophy; The Elementary and Constitutional Principles of the Municipal Law of England, and herein, Of the Feudal Law, The Institutes of the Municipal Law Generally, The Origin and Progress of the Common Law; The Law of Real Rights and Real Remedies; The Law of Personal Rights and Personal Remedies; The Law of Equity; The Lex Mercatoria; The Law of Crimes and Their Punishments; The Law of Nations; The Maritime and Admiralty Law; The Civil or Roman Law; The Constitution and Laws of the United States of America, and herein of the Jurisdiction and Practice of the Courts of the United States; Comparative Jurisprudence, and the Constitutions and Laws of the Several States of the Union; and Political Economy.
>
> "*Resolved,* That the said state and other local bar associations be respectfully requested to recommend and further in such law schools, the *requirement of attendance on at least the studies and exercises appointed for said course of three years, as a qualification for examination to be admitted to the bar.*" [Emphasis added]

Shades of Blackstone, Hoffman and others appear before us! Like Banquo's ghost they will not down. These resolutions were laid on the table. The bar was not yet ready for moves of this sort.

Another highlight among the annual reports of the committee was that made in 1891. Simeon E. Baldwin was President of the Association that year. The report of the committee was made by its chairman, William G. Hammond of Missouri. Henry Wade Rogers, then President of Northwestern University, was a member of the committee.[7] The report covers sixty pages. The committee had done a tremendous job in gathering statistical data on law schools and law students. This, it should be noted, was a new and significant vehicle of information in this area. But quite beyond its impressive array of factual materials, the report was a major plea for improvements in legal education. "If the profession is now careless of the subject," warned the committee,[8]

> "and looks upon education for the Bar as a matter that only interests the beginner and his teachers, this sentiment is the most convincing proof of its blindness to its own defects, and to the close connection between these and the defects of the law schools. No lesson has been more clearly taught by the history of our science from the beginning than that, wherever the law has been best administered and most truly worthy of its high mission, its votaries have been most careful of the education of students and in the statement of its principles, so that such students could thoroughly master them."

The report did not receive the attention it deserved nor were the resolutions proposed by the committee voted on by the Association. Because of the lateness of the hour when this item came up for consideration, it was recommitted to the committee. Apparently another major effort of the committee had come to naught. This may not, however, be a valid assumption. Of concrete actions on the part of the

---

[7] Years later, in 1911–1912, the writer was a student in a class in the Yale Law School taught by Simeon E. Baldwin. Judge Baldwin was then Governor of Connecticut. The Dean of the Law School at that time was Henry Wade Rogers.

[8] 14 Rep. Am. Bar Ass'n, 301, 320–321 (1891).

Association, the committee had little of accomplishment to show. Notwithstanding, the committee had made progress, particularly in gaining the good will and support of discerning members of the bar. A statement by Judge John F. Dillon is indicative. "I wish to say," said he in commenting on the 1891 report before the action to recommit was taken,[9] "that I have taken the time since I came here to read that report in full, and I desire to state that it is my deliberate conviction that if this Association in the ten or twelve years of its existence had done nothing more than to secure that report and the very able one on the same subject that preceded it a few years ago, it would have been enough to have justified our existence."

The following year the committee was more fortunate. Again it presented an able report.[10] During the previous year it had studied the programs of instruction of the various law schools, and had carried on an extensive correspondence on the subject of legal education with law-school teachers and members of the bar. It analyzed the case method and presented arguments for and against it. After submitting its report, the committee moved the approval of a number of resolutions, which, after debate and some modification, were adopted by the Association.[11] Among the resolutions adopted were the following:

> "That the American Bar Association strongly recommend that the power of admitting members to the Bar, and the supervision of their professional conduct, be in each State lodged in the highest courts of the State; . . .
>
> "That at least two years of study should be required of every student before he presents himself for examination; . . .

---

[9] *Ibid.*, 49.

[10] 15 Rep. Am. Bar Ass'n, 317 (1892). John F. Dillon was president of the Association that year.

[11] *Ibid.*, 8–20.

> "That, in the opinion of this Association, it is a part of the highest duty and interest of every civilized State to make provisions when necessary for the maintenance of law-schools, and the thorough professional education of all who are admitted to practice law."

Another resolution submitted by the committee on this occasion and approved by the Association also merits mention because it involved action that foreshadowed a significant movement in legal education which only recently has gotten under way. This resolution was to the effect that all law schools should, if possible, maintain programs of post-graduate instruction for lawyers, and particularly for young lawyers. As the committee conceived these courses, they were to provide instruction in those branches of the law which were necessarily excluded from the work required for the degree. This discerning recommendation did not take root immediately. It was not until the 1930's that measures of this sort were initiated and not until after World War II that they came to fruition, through the development of the continuing legal education programs currently sponsored by the American Law Institute and vigorously pressed by some bar associations and some law schools.

C. THE "JOHN MARSHALL" AND "ABRAHAM LINCOLN" ARGUMENT

One objection that was perennially advanced against moves to promote the cause of legal education centered on the poor boy who was unable to meet the expense of a long period of training for the bar, and particularly the expense of a law-school education. It was a remnant of "Jacksonian democracy," but its roots were deeper than that. Often, to be sure, there were reasons for suspecting the motivations of those who advanced the argument. It is a mistake, however, to put all who took this position into that category, for some spoke from genuine conviction. The objection is sometimes referred to as the "John Marshall," and again as the "Abraham Lincoln," argument. It appeared at the very beginning of the debates in the Association. It has periodically been advanced in the debates that followed, up to very recent years. It has been one of the main obstacles that has retarded the development of legal education.

In 1880, when the recommendations of the Hunt Committee were under consideration, Hinkley of Maryland spoke in opposition. "There are men in this country," he contended,[12] "who may not be able to pay for a law school education, who yet may be ornaments to their profession in the future. For this reason I think no resolution ought to be adopted by this body looking to a diploma as an essential qualification." Said Potter of New York in 1892, when the resolutions of the Hammond Committee were debated:[13] "To deny the privilege to a class of young men who are not among the poorest students, or, if they enter the bar, not generally among the poorest lawyers in the land, who have not the means for another year's study, I think, is unwise." "I recollect," commented Hitchcock of Missouri,[14] "if I am not very much mistaken, that the biographer of Chief-Justice Marshall says that he attended one course of law lectures in William and Mary College." Budd of Pennsylvania spoke in reply. He was contending that the period of preparation should be three years. "Why should we here claim," said he,[15]

> "that three years is too much to ask of the average young man before coming to the bar? Take the case of Chief-Justice Marshall—take the case of another Virginian, Patrick Henry, who is supposed to have read law six

[12] 3 Rep. Am. Bar Ass'n, 42 (1880).
[13] 15 Rep. Am. Bar Ass'n, 14 (1892).
[14] *Ibid.*, 15.
[15] *Ibid.*, 18.

weeks. They were exceptional men. Exceptional men will arise in every profession and at every time. But legislation must be for the general man."

D. THE FORMATION OF THE SECTION OF LEGAL EDUCATION —EARLY PROGRAMS

Over the years until 1893 the committee had been making its reports at the general meetings of the Association. As the activities of the Association increased, the time that could be devoted at the general meetings to legal education often was inadequate and the recommendations of the committee failed to get action, not infrequently, merely because the Association was unable to give attention to them. This problem had been a matter of concern for some years to the members of the committee and others interested in legal education. In 1893 a momentous step, in the interest both of the Association and of legal education, was taken. The ground having previously been prepared, the Executive Committee of the Association that year recommended a by-law to establish "a section of the Association to be known as the Section of Legal Education." On motion of Simeon E. Baldwin the report of the Executive Committee was approved and the first section of the American Bar Association came into being.[16] This was a most significant move. The idea was to create a forum within the Association to which a substantial measure of autonomy could be delegated. The section was the answer. It was a deliberative unit that had power to elect its own officers, schedule programs, and debate and pass motions. The principal restriction was that its actions could not become those of the Association until they had been formally presented to and approved by it. Since 1893 numerous other sections have been established by the Association, and they have given substance and vigor

[16] 16 Rep. Am. Bar Ass'n, 7–10 (1893).

to its programs. For legal education this action was a life line.

The day following its organization, the new Section held its first meeting. Among the speakers who addressed that meeting was Professor Samuel Williston. The Section elected Henry Wade Rogers as its chairman.[17]

The proceedings of the Association often tell a discouraging story about the attitude of the bar on the problems of legal education; they also tell one that is quite the reverse. The proceedings disclose that many lawyers were indifferent to the implications of legal education, but they also show that this was not true of the leaders of the profession, many of whom were deeply sensitive to and enlightened on this subject. They were serious about it, and gave freely of their time to advance its cause. Their work lights up what otherwise would have been a desolate area. At a later time we shall find that Elihu Root, William Howard Taft, Harlan F. Stone, John W. Davis, William G. McAdoo, and George W. Wickersham, to mention only a few of the many who contributed, struck mighty blows for the advancement of legal education. For the moment, however, our attention centers on the meeting of the Section of Legal Education in 1894. This was the first full meeting of the Section. It was a noteworthy occasion because of the individuals who participated in the program and the excellent substance of their papers. The Chairman of the Section, Henry Wade Rogers, gave an able and informative address. The other speakers on the program and their respective topics were: John F. Dillon, who spoke on "The True Professional Ideal"; John D. Lawson, "Some Standards of Legal Education in the West"; Simeon E. Baldwin, "Law School Libraries, and How to Use Them"; Woodrow Wilson, "Legal Education of Undergraduates"; John H. Wigmore, "A Principle of Orthodox

[17] *Ibid.*, 366–409.

Legal Education"; Edmund Wetmore, "Some of the Limitations and Requirements of Legal Education in the United States"; William A. Keener, "The Inductive Method in Legal Education."[18]

This truly was a galaxy of talent. Their addresses provide the materials for an independent study. The hope is expressed that someone will accept that assignment and will lift these addresses from obscurity. They contain a vast fund of information on legal education of that period and of the past. In them is to be found a faithful expression on what the leaders of the bar and of the schools of that day thought about legal education, and a revealment of their ideals. These addresses richly deserve analysis and appraisal in the light of modern thinking and values. For the purposes of the present study we can do little more than give an impressionistic statement on them.

Chairman Rogers in his opening address reported that 72 law schools were in 1894 in operation in the United States, and that of this number all but seven were associated with universities. The enrollment in the schools for that year was 7,600; in 1870, by way of contrast, the overall number in the schools was only 1,611. Of some import was his observation that it no longer was necessary to debate the question whether the study of law in a law school was preferable to study in an office. "The Law Schools," he said,[19] "have grown immensely in the favor of the profession, and the best informed and ablest members of the profession are arrayed on their side." He pointed out that substantial advances in admission requirements to the schools had been made in the years immediately before 1894. In 1875 the schools generally specified no qualifications for admission. By 1894 Harvard had announced that after 1895–1896 no person would be ad-

[18] 17 Rep. Am. Bar Ass'n, 351–493 (1894).

[19] *Ibid.*, 389–394.

mitted as a candidate for the law degree who had not previously acquired an academic degree from one of a selected list of colleges. "It is gratifying to observe," he commented,[20] "that almost all of the schools now require applicants for admission to be possessed at least of a good elementary English education, and to have a knowledge of the history of England and the United States."

On the question of the length of the period of law-school study, the schools still varied widely in their practices. Chairman Rogers found one that was graduating students at the end of two five-month terms. Most schools prescribed two years, and a small but increasing number had established a three-year requirement. He commented favorably on the growing number of law reviews published by the schools. As to methods of instruction the schools were divided. Some still emphasized the lecture method; most used the text system; at least six by that time had adopted the case method.

One observation that ever becomes more pointed, as we follow through the long years the debates on the subject of legal education, relates to the repeated criticism by discerning members of the profession that the programs of education lacked breadth and that they were too technical. That was the main criticism of office-apprentice training. When the schools gained the ascendancy it was in turn directed against their programs. We must not assume from this that there were no advocates for practical and technical training. There were—many of them—but the thoughtful leaders of the profession pleaded for scope and perspective in education. This factor was stressed by Judge Dillon in his address. "I insist," said he,[21]

"for I believe it to be true, that the stereotyped course of

[20] *Ibid.*, 398.

[21] *The True Professional Ideal, ibid.*, 409, 420.

> legal instruction in this country is defective, not so much for what it contains as for what it omits. It is defective in that no adequate provision is made for specific instruction in historical and comparative jurisprudence, and in the literature, science and philosophy of the law—in what may, perhaps, be compendiously expressed as general jurisprudence."

"Especially do I believe in the efficacy of the study of the classics as part of the foundation of a legal training," stressed Edmund Wetmore.[22] "I know no better means for acquiring that clearness of style and facile use of the English language, which are so potent and essential in the actual practice of the profession, as the study and translation of the masterpieces of classical literature."

I have expressed the view that all of the papers read on this noteworthy occasion merit analysis and appraisal. We shall end this excursion to them with the address of Woodrow Wilson. He urged that law studies be established as a university discipline. He went further, and stressed the importance of instruction in the essential nature and processes of the law for all citizens. "We need laymen," said he,[23] "who understand the necessity for law, and the right uses of it, too well to be unduly impatient of its restraints; and lawyers who understand the necessity for reform and the safe means of effecting it, too well to be unreasonably shy of assisting it." Every businessman should have at least a minimum training in the law; every minister should know the function that law performs in society; every citizen, in fact, "should know what law is, how it came into existence, what relation its form bears to its substance, and how it gives to society its fibre and strength and poise of

[22] *Some of the Limitations and Requirements of Legal Education in the United States*, *ibid.*, 461, 462.

[23] *Legal Education of Undergraduates*, *ibid.*, 439, 441.

frame."[24] The worst enemy of the law, he emphasized,[25] "is the man who knows only its technical details and neglects its generative principles, and the worst enemy of the lawyer is the man who does not comprehend why it is that there need be any technical details at all." Thus, over a century after Blackstone delivered his famous lectures, his views on education find support, and with emphasis, in the eloquent words of a great American educator and statesman.

In 1895 James Bradley Thayer was Chairman of the Section, and Justice David J. Brewer was one of the principal speakers at its annual meeting. His subject was "A Better Education the Great Need of the Profession."[26] He spoke of the leadership, actual and potential, of the lawyer in public affairs, and of the role the lawyer should play in law improvement. If the lawyer is to measure up to these responsibilities, he emphasized, he "must be fitted to lead. . . . If our profession," he continued,[27]

> "is to maintain its prominence, if it is going to continue the great profession, that which leads and directs the movements of society, a longer course of preparatory study must be required. A better education is the great need and the most important reform. The door of admission to the bar must swing on reluctant hinges, and only he be permitted to pass through who has by continued and patient study fitted himself for the work of a safe counselor and the place of a leader."

He was familiar with the "John Marshall" and "Abraham Lincoln" argument. His reply to it was characteristically forthright. "It is said," he noted,[28]

> "that some of the noblest of our members would be shut

[24] *Ibid.*, 442.
[25] *Ibid.*, 441.
[26] 18 Rep. Am. Bar Ass'n, 441 (1895).
[27] *Ibid.*, 450.
[28] *Ibid.*, 453.

out from the law and turned into other pursuits. If a four years' course of study had been required, would Abraham Lincoln have become a lawyer? My reply is twofold. First, seldom would any one capable of becoming a hero of the bar be turned away. Obstacles only stimulate the efforts of such men. They work their way up in spite of all difficulties. They glory in their ability to overcome all opposition. Secondly, if perchance some one worthy of a place on our rolls should be kept away there will be plenty left. The general level of professional standing should not be lowered for fear some single chieftain is never found."

E. FURTHER MOVES TO STRENGTHEN LEGAL EDUCATION—CONFERENCE OF BAR EXAMINERS

The Association during the years immediately under consideration had both a Section of Legal Education and a Committee on Legal Education and Admissions to the Bar. The practice was to refer resolutions adopted by the Section to the Committee. The Committee made recommendations to the Association. In 1897, on recommendation of the Committee, the Association adopted the following resolutions:[29]

> "*Resolved,* That the American Bar Association approves the lengthening of the course of instruction in law schools to a period of three years, and that it expresses the hope that as soon as practicable a rule may be adopted in each State which will require candidates for admission to the bar to study law for three years before applying for examination.
>
> "*Resolved,* That the American Bar Association is of the opinion that before a student commences the study

[29] The Association ran into a parliamentary snarl in adopting these resolutions and there was extended debate over them. 20 Rep. Am. Bar Ass'n, 20–34 (1897).

of law, it is desirable that he should have received a general education at least equivalent to a high school course, and that persons who have not completed the equivalent of such a course should not be admitted into law schools as candidates for a degree."

It would seem that the mills of the Association on matters relating to legal education grind slowly. Even in 1897 the Association could do no more than express the view that students should have at least the equivalent of a high-school course before starting their law studies. It is true that several law schools had requirements by that time in excess of that minimum, but this does not detract from the fact that the Association felt unable as of that date to make a stronger statement.

Another point of interest in the 1897 report of the Committee relates to a clash of views among the members of the Committee on the scope of the programs offered by the law schools. A majority of the Committee criticized the schools because their courses of study were too technical and because they did not train students for a public career. The majority report acknowledged that the schools faced problems in broadening their programs, but urged, notwithstanding, that they give their attention to this question. The minority report, signed by Dean McClain, later justice of the Supreme Court of Iowa, and Professor Wambaugh, took exception to the majority view. "We should regret," reads the minority report,[30]

"to see the three years' course in law weakened by omitting some legal topics and substituting some non-legal topics, however valuable the substitutes may be,—in short, even if the substitutes should be history and political science,—and accordingly we must express dis-

[30] *Ibid.*, 383.

approval of so much of the majority report as seems to suggest or permit any substitution."

In 1898 the Section of Legal Education called a conference of the members of state boards of law examiners.[31] This conference was scheduled as a phase of the program of the Section. It was an extremely significant move on its part, for, as we have observed, the development of legal education in this country has been and will continue to be affected by the status and change in status of the standards of bar admission. While similar conferences were called in subsequent years by the Section, it was not until 1931, as Professor Sullivan has related,[32] that the National Conference of Bar Examiners as an integral unit was established. It came into being principally through the efforts of Will Shafroth, then adviser to the Section of Legal Education.

F. FORMATION OF THE ASSOCIATION OF AMERICAN LAW SCHOOLS

While a number of law-school teachers had, before the turn of the century, attended the meetings of the Section of Legal Education and had made substantial contributions to its programs, the Section was of the opinion that action should be taken to bring the law schools into closer contact with the work of the Section and with each other. In consequence, in 1899, on the motion of Henry Wade Rogers, the Section voted:[33] "That a committee of three be appointed to take into consideration what action, if any, shall be taken to bring the reputable law schools of the country into closer relations with each other and with the Section of Legal Education, and that this committee have power to invite such

[31] 21 Rep. Am. Bar Ass'n, 503 (1898).

[32] *The Professional Associations and Legal Education,* 4 J. Legal Ed. 401, 409 (1952).

[33] 22 Rep. Am. Bar Ass'n, 565 (1899).

law schools to meet in conference with the Section next year."

Pursuant to this action the committee, which the motion had authorized, sent letters to all the law schools of the country, inviting them to send representatives to the Section at its meeting in 1900. Thirty-five responded by sending delegates; in all, fifty-four individuals, as representatives of schools, were present.[34] On August 28, this group met, organized the Association of American Law Schools and adopted Articles of Association.[35] The new Association took for its object the improvement of legal education in America. The Articles went on to provide, among other things: That the schools which had delegates at the meeting and which signed the Articles before July 1, 1901, would be members of the Association, provided they complied with Article Sixth. The sixth article was the critical one. It, in substance, provided that a school was eligible for membership if it: (1) required of candidates for its degree the completion of a high-school course, or its equivalent; (2) maintained a course of study leading to its degree that covered at least two years of thirty weeks per year, provided that after 1905 a member school had to require a three years' course; (3) owned, or had convenient access to during all regular library hours, a library that contained the reports of the state in which the school was located and the reports of the Supreme Court of the United States.[36]

---

[34] 23 Rep. Am. Bar Ass'n, 447, 569–570 (1900).

[35] *Ibid.*, 569–575.

[36] When the organization of the Association of American Law Schools and the contents of the Articles of Association were reported to the Section, an extended debate took place. What was this strange creature which was the "child" of the Section, for which the Section must assume paternity, but which was not answerable for its actions to the Section? The debate centered on that part of the Sixth Article which provided that after 1905 members of the Association must require a three-year course. The debate ended by the Section's doing no more than receiving the report. *Ibid.*, 447–458.

It is to be observed that these Articles did little more than parallel the actions previously taken by the American Bar Association. There was, however, this difference: Whereas the resolutions of the American Bar Association had expressed views and opinions that were aimed to bring about results through persuasion,[37] the Articles of the Association of American Law Schools spoke with authority as to those schools which wished to maintain themselves in this select circle. Even so, in the light of present ideas about legal education, the requirements stated in the original Articles seem pitiful. What is significant is that through the organization of the Association of American Law Schools, a new and potent instrumentality for the advancement of the cause of legal education had been introduced into the scene.

G. THE PROBLEM OF PRELEGAL EDUCATION

One of the individuals who addressed the Section of Legal Education at its meeting in 1900 was William Draper Lewis, who later was to make a substantial contribution to the organization and administration of the American Law Institute. He spoke on "The Proper Preparation for the Study of Law."[38] He dealt with prelegal education. This subject was one for which lawyers and teachers alike were not yet fully prepared.[39] It is, however, one which has taken on meaning and substance in recent years. It is a curious commentary that we appear always to have viewed legal education as a phenomenon restricted to that period during which the individual actually studies law—the immediate period of his preparation for admission to the bar. We have looked upon it as an experience in the law student's life, isolated

[37] Later the Section took more aggressive actions.

[38] *Ibid.*, 475.

[39] This is evident from the discussion that followed Lewis' address. Lewis was called an idealist; also the "John Marshall" and "Abraham Lincoln" argument got another airing. *Ibid.*, 421–437.

from all other influences that contribute to his education. We seem to have missed the very pertinent fact that legal education is for the lawyer a lifetime affair. I venture the opinion that had we viewed the problems of legal education in a broader perspective, we would have made more intelligent progress with them. Clearly, it would seem, pre-law-school education is an important phase of the overall education of a lawyer.

Lewis recognized the significance of the movement to require college work as a condition to entering upon the study of law. He did not disparage this development. He assumed that college work was essential. His address centered on the substance of the college work. He contended that law schools should do more than set up prelegal requirements; that they should also specify courses and fields of knowledge that had meaning and educational content for the prospective law student. "A preparatory education," he argued,[40] "should seek to prepare the mind for the real work which the mind will be called upon to do."

We have been dealing in this study with two contentions that have been advanced in connection with legal education that are closely related but which need to be distinguished. Actually, both stem from a common source but they have branched off until now they appear to be quite independent. One centers on the views expressed by Blackstone and some of the men who held the early professorships of law in America, that programs of legal instruction should be liberalized and that they should present to the student a broad synthesis of law in the setting of its interrelations with other disciplines—with government, history, and economics. This essentially has also been the conception of legal education that has prevailed in the continental countries of Europe. These views were advanced in England and America in re-

[40] *Ibid.*, 478.

action to the restricted technical system of education that was current at that time in both countries. When legal education in America gravitated to the universities, the criticism of the limited content of the course of instruction was still valid. The universities offered better teaching than the offices, but beyond that they merely substituted one technical program for another. The introduction of the case system worked no substantial change. In some respects case instruction confined legal education into an even narrower mold.

The second contention is more recent in origin. It too arose in reaction against the restricted content of the course of law instruction. It manifested itself in the movement to set up prelegal requirements for admission to the law schools and to the bar. In a substantial measure when college work was prescribed as a condition precedent to law study, legal education was liberalized. This movement, however, did not contemplate, or at least it did not as it was first conceived, broadening the scope of the instruction offered by the law schools.

From these premises added substance and meaning may, perhaps, be found in what Lewis was feeling for. His position essentially was that the law schools should require not only a period of college study as a prerequisite for admission but that they should also designate the content of the college work taken. That is, he argued against the mere prescription of college work as a hit-or-miss affair. He contended that the college work should have direction and meaning for the student; that the overall program of college and law-school work should have unity and synthesis. This may be reading more into Lewis' remarks than he intended, but be that as it may, this rationalization presents an inviting subject for reflection. A planned overall program, properly coordinated, of college and law-school work would tend to bring the two diverging developments just described into a common focus. It would tend to bring to a rich fulfillment the conception of the great pioneers in legal education of the late seventeen and early eighteen hundreds.

The question of pre-law-school education is still in the doldrums today. It is a valid criticism of the law schools and of the bar that they have done little on this important subject. Whenever the question of college work as a prerequisite to admission to law study has arisen, the emphasis has been on quantity—on how many credit hours should be required. "It is strange," observed Professor Sullivan,[41] "that although from the very beginning of the American Bar Association, prelegal college training received consideration and discussion and its importance was restated almost annually, no specific recommendation was made until 1921 and then only on the quantity of college work to be required prior to entrance to law school." Others have commented on this inaction of the schools and with even greater emphasis. "The time has come, gentlemen," stressed a great university president in an address before the American Bar Association,[42] "for the schools of law to say that they wish their incoming students to come to them, having pursued, systematically and well, those studies in the field of economics and history and social science that will prepare them to understand the fundamental concepts of the law, their development and their application." In 1935 the Association of American Law Schools gave some attention to the quality of the college work acceptable for admission to law school by adding a sentence to its Articles reading: "Such work must have been passed with a scholastic average at least equal to the average required for graduation in the institutions at-

---

[41] *The Professional Associations and Legal Education,* 4 J. Legal Ed. 401, 408 (1952).

[42] Butler, *Preliminary Education for Law Students,* 8 A.B.A. Jour. 684, 685 (1922).

tended."[43] But neither that Association nor the American Bar Association has come to grips with problems of defining the substance and content of the college work taken.[44]

H. DEVELOPMENTS, 1903–1913

In 1903 the law school Association approved a recommendation of its Executive Committee which instructed that Committee "to investigate and report whether any members of the Association fall short of the requirements of article sixth of the Articles of Association."[45] This action in the light of subsequent developments was a significant one. It meant that the schools in the Association were open to more than a paper check relative to their compliance with the standards of the Association; they were subject to inspections. At the present time inspections are common both by the Association of American Law Schools and the American Bar Association.

Over the years the Association of American Law Schools, on various occasions, has stimulated and given its support to scholarly enterprises. In 1905 the Association adopted a resolution that was submitted by Dean Wigmore, which authorized a committee to investigate the feasibility of publishing translations of foreign works of legal scholarship and of original research in legal history.[46] This resolution found fulfillment in the course of a few years in the

---

[43] Handbook, Ass'n Am. L. Schools, 11 (1935). One of the studies made for the Survey deals with this subject: Crotty, *Who Shall Be Called to the Bar?* 20 Bar Exam. 173 (1951).

[44] Two excellent studies have been made by Chief Justice Arthur T. Vanderbilt: the first, A Report on Prelegal Education, pamph. (1944), made to the American Bar Association; the second, *A Report on Prelegal Education*, 25 N. Y. U. L. Rev. 199 (1950), made to the Survey. The present Committee on Pre-Legal Education of the Association of American Law Schools is devoting attention to this subject. We shall make mention of its work later.

[45] Handbook, Ass'n Am. L. Schools, 9 (1903).

[46] Handbook, Ass'n Am. L. Schools, 15–18 (1905).

publication of *Select Essays in Anglo-American Legal History, The Continental Legal History Series*, and *The Modern Legal Philosophy Series*. These works have been of invaluable aid to scholarship in this country.

In accordance with the action taken when the Association of American Law Schools adopted its Articles of Association at its organizational meeting in 1900, the three-year requirement for law study went into effect in 1906. Also in 1906, Roscoe Pound addressed the American Bar Association on "The Causes of Popular Dissatisfaction with the Administration of Justice."[47] This address had wide repercussions and was influential in shaking the profession out of its apathy on matters of law improvement. In 1907 Pound was Chairman of the Section of Legal Education of the American Bar Association. His address delivered at the annual meeting of the Section on "The Need of a Sociological Jurisprudence" was another of his noteworthy performances.[48]

The Committee on Legal Education and Admissions to the Bar, which notwithstanding the organization of the Section of Legal Education and of the Association of American Law Schools continued to function, and which in past years had made a number of extremely able reports to the American Bar Association, produced in 1907 another masterpiece.[49] The report was presented to the Association by Henry Wade Rogers. John H. Wigmore and Joseph H. Beale, Jr., were on the Committee.[50] The

[47] 29 Rep. Am. Bar Ass'n, 395 (1906).

[48] 31 Rep. Am. Bar Ass'n, 911 (1907).

[49] *Ibid.*, 518.

[50] That the rank-and-file members of the American Bar Association were not yet ready for the implications of the Committee's report is evidenced by the discussion that followed its presentation. *Ibid.*, 64–68. Professor Beale dissented from the report, in part. *Ibid.*, 599.

Committee reported that as of that date, 1907, there were seventy-four law schools in the United States that had a three-year course of study; thirty-six had a two-year course; and two had a one-year course. Relative to bar admissions the Committee said twenty-three states and territories had prescribed a three-year course of law study; ten had prescribed two years; one had a requirement of one year; and eighteen had fixed no period of study whatever. The case system was used exclusively at that time in ten law schools. In nineteen others it was the chief but not the exclusive method of instruction. The committee devoted attention to the problem of night schools. It reported that thirty night schools were in operation, of which only four were then conducting a four-year course. It gave its approval to the night-school idea, but was of the opinion that a standard of four years of study should be established for all night schools. It severely condemned the study of law by correspondence. As many as twelve correspondence law schools were then in operation.[51]

In 1913 the Committee on Legal Education and Admissions to the Bar reported to the American Bar Association that it had requested the Carnegie Foundation for the Advancement of Teaching to undertake a study of legal education in the United States.[52] The committee commented on the excellent report on medical education that had been published in 1910, and expressed the view "that the greatest possible service could be rendered to the law schools and the Bar if the Carnegie Foundation could be induced to undertake the work and do for legal education what it did for medical education."[53] The response from the Founda-

[51] The present status of correspondence law study is covered in a report prepared for the Survey of the Legal Profession, Pierce, *Correspondence Law Schools*, 4 J. Legal Ed. 160 (1951).

[52] 38 Rep. Am. Bar Ass'n, 25, 474 (1913).

[53] *Ibid.*, 475.

tion was favorable. "The Foundation," the committee reported,[54]

> "has explained that it intends that the study shall cover not only the examination of all the law schools of the country, of the various curriculums of study and of their libraries and facilities for teaching, but that it hopes to bring under consideration the relation of the legal profession to the administration of the law and to the obligations of the social regime. An effort is to be made to trace the evolution of the legal profession in the United States and its relation to legislation and administration and of the relation of the number of lawyers to the amount of litigation and the cost of the legal process."

This move resulted in the publication in 1914 of the Redlich report, *The Common Law and the Case Method in American University Law Schools,* and later, also under the aegis of the Carnegie Foundation, of two reports by A. Z. Reed, *Training for the Public Profession of the Law,* in 1921, and *Present-Day Law Schools in the United States and Canada,* in 1928. All three were reports ably executed and highly informative. It was not, however, until the current Survey of the Legal Profession, also supported in part by the Carnegie Corporation, that the hopes expressed by the Foundation as described by the Committee, relative to a comprehensive study covering not only legal education but the legal profession as well, were given promise of fulfillment.

I. THE SEPARATION OF THE AALS FROM THE ABA

Another action, this by the Association of American Law Schools, taken in 1913, was to be of considerable import

[54] *Ibid.*, 476.

to legal education. Ever since its organization in 1900 that Association had held its annual meetings at the time and place of the annual meetings of the American Bar Association. And since the meetings of the bar association were set primarily to meet the convenience of practicing lawyers, and not that of law teachers, this often caused problems relative to the attendance of the teachers. As a consequence the meetings of the law school Association were at times poorly attended. Also, some feeling had developed among the teachers that the time allotted to their meetings did not allow for adequate discussions of law-school problems. At the 1913 meeting of the law school Association, its Executive Committee proposed a resolution that it be the sense of the Association that it should hold a special meeting in the following winter or spring "to give opportunity for a thorough discussion of some one or more subjects of interest to" its members.[55] After discussion, a substitute motion was passed "that the whole question of the advisability of changing the date of meeting by constitutional amendment be referred to the Executive Committee and duly reported to the next meeting."[56] Then came the decisive factor. The American Bar Association scheduled its 1914 meeting for the latter part of October, which was a time quite impossible for attendance on the part of most law-school people.

The Executive Committee acted quickly and drastically, but, as Professor Seavey has said, "in accordance with the legal tradition."[57] The fourteenth annual meeting of the Association of American Law Schools met in Chicago in December 1914 during the Christmas holidays. Secretary Walter Wheeler Cook explained the circumstances which

[55] Handbook, Ass'n Am. L. Schools, 18 (1913).

[56] *Ibid.*, 20–21.

[57] *The Association of American Law Schools in Retrospect*, 3 J. Legal Ed. 153, 160 (1950).

led up to that meeting. "The committee," said he,[58] "were confronted this year by the fact that the Bar Association seceded from us, so to speak, as they decided to hold their meeting in October, just after the law schools had all begun their work." If the Association was to have any respectable attendance at its annual meeting, it had to be scheduled at another time. There was, however, this problem: The Articles of the Association required the Association to meet with the Bar Association. The committee found a solution. A formal meeting of the Association was called in October, at the time the American Bar Association met. This meeting was forthwith adjourned to meet again in Chicago in December. At the December meeting the Articles of Association were amended to read:[59] "The Association shall meet annually at the time and place at which the American Bar Association meets, unless the Executive Committee shall otherwise direct." As revealed by subsequent events, the separation of the Association of American Law Schools from its parent organization, the American Bar Association, was complete.

What were the implications of this move? The Association of American Law Schools, it would appear, both gained and lost by it. Unquestionably, it resulted in a greater measure of freedom for this group. There was apparent something of a feeling of emancipation about the 1914 meeting. Three days were scheduled for that meeting, with the result that the discussions were unhurried and deliberative. The round tables, which have proved to be a very valuable adjunct to the programs of the Association, were initiated that year. Though it is not clear that those who participated in it realized its full import, the action taken in 1914 created an independent entity. Thus, the Association gained a more favorable climate for the develop-

[58] Handbook, Ass'n Am. L. Schools, 11 (1914).
[59] *Ibid.*, 8–14.

ment of its own programs than would have been possible had it continued its close relations with the American Bar Association.

But the step taken by the Association in 1914 also had prejudicial implications, for it tended to widen an already existing gulf between law teachers and the members of the practicing bar. Law teaching as a profession came into being at Harvard with Langdell. Before Langdell law teachers were drawn from the ranks of the practicing bar, and though teachers, they remained essentially practitioners. Langdell insisted on a staff of full-time instructors. Other law schools followed Harvard's lead and so there came into existence a group of lawyers who devoted their time exclusively to teaching and legal scholarship. These individuals today constitute a distinct branch of the legal profession. The advent of this group was a major and most salutary innovation for legal education. It produced a small but select class of men who devoted their entire time to legal education—to teaching and legal research. This development lifted law teaching from the trade-school level to a respected university discipline.

Associated with this movement, however, there developed a tendency, apparent from the time of its inception, for the law teacher to separate himself from the practicing profession and its affairs, and to move in a distinct orbit. Some of the men who were present at the 1914 meeting, and particularly John H. Wigmore and William R. Vance, had a sense of foreboding that the action contemplated by the Association would accentuate this tendency. "I think," said Vance,[60] "all of us realize that it will be a fatal blunder for the law teachers of this country ever to sever their intimate and close relation with the Bar of the country." For a time after 1914 the gulf between the teachers

[60] *Ibid.*, 9.

and the practicing bar did, in fact, widen and to the distinct disadvantage of both groups. It was not until recent years that this separation was substantially bridged.

What must be apparent is that it is neither expedient nor desirable for law teachers to isolate themselves from the ongoing work of the practicing bar. Quite the reverse: an intimate insight into the workings of the law—an understanding of the problems men seek to solve through law and a discernment as to the defects in the machinery of the law, coupled with an ability to project designs for its improvement—is essential for the law teacher if he is to travel the paths of reality in either his teaching or his research. This view found able expression in a report of a committee of the Harvard Law School. "Effective scholarship," observed the committee,[61]

> "cannot thrive in isolation from reality, and one of the most significant realities of law and government lies in the existence of the legal profession itself,—a profession with traditions and standards and a force of its own in the affairs of men. The School must maintain its intimate contact with that profession, and that contact is at least as important to its program of research as it is to its course of professional training. . . . For good or ill, the legal scholar must find his salvation as a member of the legal profession, sharing its traditions and aims, and sharing a responsibility not only for the improvement of the law, but for the advancement of the profession as well."

In 1914 Wesley Newcomb Hohfeld spoke to the Association of American Law Schools on the topic "A Vital School of Jurisprudence and Law."[62] It was a notable address.

---

61 Preliminary Statement of the Committee on Legal Education of the Harvard Law School, 4–5 (1947).

62 Handbook, Ass'n Am. L. Schools, 76 (1914).

From it stemmed the organization of the American Law Institute. We shall return to a discussion of this address later. In 1916 Elihu Root was president of the American Bar Association. A substantial portion of his address, "Public Service by the Bar,"[63] was devoted to legal education and admissions to the bar. He stressed the public responsibilities of lawyers. If the profession is to meet its public obligations, he contended, it must have better educated lawyers. To that end he advocated the initiation of measures that would screen from admission to the bar incompetent and poorly prepared individuals. "No one," said he,[64]

> "can help sympathizing with the idea that every ambitious young American should have an opportunity to win fame and fortune. But that should not be the controlling consideration here. The controlling consideration should be the public service, and the right to win the rewards of the profession should be conditioned upon fitness to render the public service. No incompetent sailor is entitled to command a public ship; no incompetent engineer is entitled to construct a public work; no untrained lawyer is entitled to impair the efficiency of the great and costly machinery which the people of the country provide, not for the benefit of lawyers but for the administration of the law."

J. RESOLUTIONS OF ABA IN 1921; INFLUENCE OF ELIHU ROOT

Events were now beginning to take shape for another major blow by the American Bar Association on behalf of legal education. In 1917 the Association created a Council on Legal Education to replace its Committee on Legal Education and Admissions to the Bar.[65] In 1919, it adopted a

[63] 41 Rep. Am. Bar Ass'n, 355 (1916).

[64] *Ibid.*, 362.

[65] 42 Rep. Am. Bar Ass'n, 90–95 (1917). In its action on this

new Constitution which eliminated the Council but which retained the Section under the comprehensive title: Section of Legal Education and Admissions to the Bar.[66] In 1920 the Section elected Elihu Root its chairman. At the close of that meeting, on motion of William Draper Lewis, the Section adopted the following resolution:[67]

> "The Chairman for the ensuing year and six other members of the Section appointed by him shall be a special committee, which committee shall report to the next annual meeting of the Section their recommendations in respect to what, if any, action shall be taken by this Section and by the American Bar Association to create conditions which will tend to strengthen the character and improve the efficiency of persons to be admitted to the practice of law."

The election of Elihu Root as Chairman of the Section and his appointment as Chairman of this special committee were indeed master strokes.

The following year the Special Committee made a report[68] which is one of the milestones in the evolution of legal education. The Committee pointed out that there were no clear criteria bearing on the qualifications of applicants for admission to the bar. Opportunity for the individual, for his growth and development, was a factor that should not be ignored. But that should not be the controlling consideration. What then should that consideration be? A significant feature of the report is that the Committee unerringly put its stress on the vital issue. On the question

---

subject the Association got into a parliamentary snarl and it is not clear that the by-law that created the Committee was formally repealed.

66 44 Rep. Am. Bar Ass'n, 88–89, 121–131 (1919). The name of the Section had been Section of Legal Education.

67 45 Rep. Am. Bar Ass'n, 465–466 (1920).

68 46 Rep. Am. Bar Ass'n, 679 (1921).

of who should be admitted to the bar, the public interests were paramount, and the profession had not safeguarded those interests. "Most of our people," stressed the report,[69] "in their search for legal assistance, have nothing to guide them except the certificate of admission to practise issued by authority of law." But this certificate was not reliable. "Both good and bad lawyers are in active practise, and no adequate machinery has been devised to enable the uninformed client to distinguish the good from the bad." This, said the Committee,[70] "is unfair to the public, and it is unfair to all the members of the profession, because the reputation of all the members suffers for the sins of a minority." Who was responsible for this situation? The answer of the Committee was forthright. "The evil exists because the public does not understand the need for protection, and because the bar does not shoulder its moral responsibility."[71]

The punch lines in the report were in the resolutions. These were first presented to the Section of Legal Education and Admissions to the Bar. The Committee moved that the Section direct its Chairman, Mr. Root, to offer the following resolutions to the American Bar Association:[72]

"1. The American Bar Association is of the opinion that every candidate for admission to the bar should give evidence of graduation from a law school complying with the following standards:

(a) It shall require as a condition of admission at least two years of study in a college.

(b) It shall require its students to pursue a course of three years duration if they devote substantially all of their working time to their studies, and a

[69] *Ibid.*, 680.
[70] *Ibid.*
[71] *Ibid.*, 681.
[72] *Ibid.*, 687–688.

longer course, equivalent in the number of working hours, if they devote only part of their working time to their studies.

(c) It shall provide an adequate library available for the use of the students.

(d) It shall have among its teachers a sufficient number giving their entire time to the school to insure actual personal acquaintance and influence with the whole student body.

"2. The American Bar Association is of the opinion that graduation from a law school should not confer the right of admission to the bar, and that every candidate should be subjected to an examination by public authority to determine his fitness.

"3. The Council on Legal Education and Admissions to the Bar[73] is directed to publish from time to time the names of those law schools which comply with the above standards and of those which do not and to make such publications available so far as possible to intending law students.

"4. The president of the Association and the Council on Legal Education and Admissions to the Bar are directed to cooperate with the state and local bar associations to urge upon the duly constituted authorities of the several states the adoption of the above requirements for admission to the bar.

"5. The Council on Legal Education and Admissions to the Bar is directed to call a Conference on Legal Education in the name of The American Bar Association, to which the state and local bar associations shall be invited to send delegates, for the purpose of uniting the bodies represented in an effort to create conditions

[73] The reference here is to the Council of the Section of Legal Education and Admissions to the Bar, which Council had previously been created.

> favorable to the adoption of the principles above set forth."

These resolutions were adopted by the Section[74] and were forthwith presented to and approved by the American Bar Association.[75] Thus, in a rapid succession of events, culminating in the adoption of the resolutions by the American Bar Association, that organization took the most articulate and positive action on legal education ever taken in America. At the center of this movement was the commanding figure of Elihu Root, but he was not wanting in support from other powerful men. These were no mere resolutions; they projected an ongoing campaign for the improvement of legal education and the raising of standards of admission to the bar. The Council of the Section of Legal Education and Admissions to the Bar was given the assignment of publishing, from time to time, a list of approved and unapproved schools. But bar admission is, in the main, a question of state authority. The resolutions contemplated that fact. If progress was to be made, the good will and cooperation of the various state and local bar associations had to be secured. To that end the resolutions authorized the calling, in the name of the American Bar Association, of a Conference on Legal Education, to which Conference the separate state and local associations were to be invited to send delegates. To assure continuity in the carrying out of the measures set up by the resolutions, the President of the Association and the Council of the Section of Legal Education were directed to urge the constituted authorities on bar admission to press for the adoption of the projected standards in their respective jurisdictions.

In the scheme of legal education contemplated by the resolutions, there was a place for the part-time school. Mr.

---

[74] 46 Rep. Am. Bar Ass'n, 657–678 (1921).

[75] *Ibid.*, 37–47.

Root's views on this subject are pertinent. "The principle of opportunity for all," he observed,[76]

> "applies peculiarly to admission to the legal profession . . . To confine the right to practise law to one economic group would be to deny to other economic groups their just participation in the making and declaring of law. Such a restriction would properly be resented by the public . . . But in recognizing the necessity for afternoon and evening schools we do not recognize the propriety of permitting such schools to operate with low educational standards. We should not license a badly educated man to practise law simply because he has been too poor to get a good education. On the contrary, the democratic necessity for afternoon and evening schools compels a lifting of these schools to the highest standards which they can be expected to reach. Therefore we advocate requiring a longer course in these schools, equivalent in the number of working hours to a three years course in a full-time school."

There was, indeed, vigorous resistance to the action taken, first in the Section and then before the Association. An articulate spokesman for the opposition was Dean Edward T. Lee of the John Marshall Law School of Chicago. "The effect of the adoption of the recommendations," said he, in speaking before the Section,[77]

> "would be to place the control of legal education through the country in the hands of the deans of a few large day law schools who have the fate of law teachers in their hands. It would close the profession of the law to all save the leisure class of youth with means sufficient to obtain college and law school training, and

[76] *Ibid.*, 685.
[77] *Ibid.*, 668.

would bar hundreds of naturally well-endowed, zealous and industrious youths from attaining an honorable ambition. It would result, in large communities, in the establishment of legal factories with a few lawyers at the head and all others mere clerks, cut off from the hope of entering the profession. Finally it would discourage legal education throughout the country, decrease legal knowledge everywhere, and deprive masses of people in our large cities, many of them of foreign extraction, from access to our courts and legal aid for want of lawyers familiar with their language and distinctive customs."

Later he was again to speak on this subject, and in opposition to the standards, when, in 1929, this issue once more came before the Association in heated debate.[78]

K. CONFERENCE OF BAR ASSOCIATION DELEGATES IN 1922

Pursuant to the action taken by the Association, a Conference of Bar Association Delegates was held in Washington, D. C., in February 1922.[79] It was a proceeding extraordinary. Forty-four state bar associations, over one hundred local associations, two Canadian bar associations, and a number of universities were represented.[80] Clarence N. Goodwin was chairman of the Conference. Among the speakers were William Howard Taft, then Chief Justice of the Supreme Court, Elihu Root, George W. Wickersham, John W. Davis, William G. McAdoo, Samuel Williston, Herbert S. Hadley, George Wharton Pepper, and Silas H. Strawn. Two days were devoted to the meeting. The sole question under consideration was legal education. The

---

78 54 Rep. Am. Bar Ass'n, 612 (1929).

79 47 Rep. Am. Bar Ass'n, 482 (1922).

80 *Conference on Legal Education,* 8 A.B.A. Jour. 137, 138 (1922).

minutes of the Conference, as published in the Reports of the American Bar Association, record:[81] "A very enthusiastic meeting of the Conference of Delegates was held in the City of Washington on February 23 and 24, 1922, to consider the subject of improving the standards of legal education." The discussion centered on the resolutions passed by the American Bar Association at its 1921 meeting, but ranged over a much wider area.

The "John Marshall" and "Abraham Lincoln" argument again came in for a thorough airing. Commented the *American Bar Association Journal* editorially:[82]

> "The American Bar Association displayed courage and optimism when it committed to a conference of delegates of state and local bar associations, the success or failure of its project for higher educational prerequisites for admission to the bar . . .
>
> "Some there were who approached the debate with the idea that the rights of the American boy were involved and that nothing should under any circumstances be done to hinder his easy access to the bar as a means of livelihood and an opportunity for political preferment. One could see this argument melt away, when it was challenged with the declaration of the right of the public to demand safeguards against the consequences of ignorance and unfitness on the part of those who were given the right to become a part of the judicial institution and to participate in the administration of justice. The American boy does not have to practice law and has no right to exercise the lawyer's high prerogative merely as a means of personal advantage. This right is inseparably bound

---

81 47 Rep. Am. Bar Ass'n, 482 (1922).

82 *Legal Education,* 8 A.B.A. Jour. 160 (1922).

up with a duty to make himself competent for effective service to his client, to the public, to the court and to the law."

"What is all this for?" inquired Elihu Root in his address to the Conference. "What is the vital consideration underlying all the efforts of the American Bar? We are commissioned," he went on to say,

> "by the state to render a service. What we have been talking about is the way of ascertaining or of producing competency to render that service. Upon what standard of judgment shall we consider and attempt to do that? Of our rights? Of the rights of the young men who come here crowding the gates of our Bar? Is it a privilege to be passed around, a benefit to be conferred? Is there any doubt that that standard is inadmissible? Do we not all reject it?
>
> "The standard of public service is the standard of the Bar, if the Bar is to live; the maintenance of justice, the rendering of justice to rich and poor alike; prompt, inexpensive, efficient justice."[83]

"It goes without saying," stated Chief Justice Taft, "that the best preparation for the successful study and practice of such a profession is a wide and thorough general education. The best general education," he stressed,

> "is to be had at our colleges and universities. There one studies literature, language, mathematics, science, history, economics and government. . . . For no learned profession . . . is a thorough and general college education more necessary than for that of the law."[84]

Toward the end of the sessions Mr. Root arose once more

[83] 47 Rep. Am. Bar Ass'n, 495–496 (1922).

[84] *Ibid.*, 497–498.

to speak from the floor. Substitute resolutions had been introduced which if passed would have brought to naught the work of the Conference. The substitute, said he, "is accompanied by a pious hope, a resolution wholly ineffective to cure anything, just such as we have been having for a quarter of a century before the American Bar Association finally came to a concrete conclusion, which, if adopted, will accomplish something . . . do not let us stultify ourselves," he urged. "I hope sincerely," he concluded,

> "that this Conference of men who hold dear the good name and the prosperity and the moral qualities of the communities and states from which they come, will not here vote to stop the only effort the Bar has ever made to answer the prayers of the good people who want our country better, and to answer the terrible responsibility that rests upon it to maintain the free institutions which are to perpetuate liberty and order in our dear country.
>
> "All that the opposition here comes to is simply to stop, to stop! to do nothing! stop the American Bar Association, disapprove them, tell them they should do nothing! How much better, instead of beating over the prejudices and memories of a past that is gone, it is to take dear old Edward Everett Hale's maxim, 'Look forward, not back; look upward, not down, and lend a hand.' "[85]

At the end, when the Conference voted, the substitute motions were defeated and the motion on the main resolutions was approved.[86] These resolutions endorsed the standards of legal education that had been set up by the American Bar Association. They went further and made additional pronouncements. Two of these were as follows:[87]

[85] *Ibid.*, 582–584.
[86] *Ibid.*, 482–484, 584.
[87] *Ibid.*, 483.

> "Further, we believe that law schools should not be operated as commercial enterprises, and that the compensation of any officer or member of its [sic] teaching staff should not depend on the number of students or on the fees received . . .
>
> "Since the legal profession has to do with the administration of the law, and since public officials are chosen from its ranks more frequently than from the ranks of any other profession or business, it is essential that the legal profession should not become the monopoly of any economic class."

This was a glorious victory in the development of legal education. But its achievement required heroic measures and words and the combined efforts of the leaders of the American bar to dispel the accumulated preconceptions and prejudices on this subject which through the years had darkened the minds of the rank and file of the profession. The distinguished men who fought this battle accomplished their objectives, but in acclaiming their achievement may we also remember the great champions of legal education of the past, whose ideas were akin to those of the men of 1922, who also fought and who often fought in vain. The unanimity of view held by the leaders of the profession from one generation to the next over the long reach of history is a striking phenomenon. Emphases have varied but the kinship of their ideas and ideals is unmistakable.

L. PROGRESSIVE STEPS IN LEGAL EDUCATION SINCE 1922

In 1923 the Council of the Section of Legal Education and Admissions to the Bar published in two classifications its first list of approved schools.[88] Thirty-nine schools were named as then complying with the standards of the Amer-

[88] *Law Schools Meet Association Standards,* 9 A.B.A. Jour. 728 (1923).

ican Bar Association. These were placed in Class "A." Nine additional schools, which had announced an intention of complying with the standards in the "immediate future" were listed in Class "B." The Council reported it had not yet been able to secure sufficient information about the various other schools to publish the names of unapproved schools.[89] The responsibilities which the Association had placed on the Council, and particularly those relating to the publishing of the names of approved and unapproved schools, were exceedingly onerous. It was inevitable that it would need the services of a competent full-time man. In its report to the Association in 1927 the Council stated[90] it was of the opinion that "the duties placed upon it by the Association can only be properly discharged by the engagement of someone competent and conversant with such work, and giving it his entire time, whose duty it shall be to visit law schools, state and local bar associations, boards of law examiners, and others, to promote these standards by explaining the desirability of their adoption and securing the aid of those who will actively interest themselves in their establishment in the several states." The American Bar Association, the report concluded, "has a grave responsibility in these matters. The work is educational in the broadest sense. It concerns the foundations upon which the profession is built."

Mr. Silas H. Strawn, Chairman of the Section, made the report to the Association. He moved that the Association authorize the appropriation of a sum of money for the employment of an "executive force" to carry out this program. On the approval of this motion,[91] the Council forthwith created the position of "Advisor" and to that position

[89] 49 Rep. Am. Bar Ass'n, 395 (1924).

[90] 52 Rep. Am. Bar Ass'n, 340 (1927).

[91] *Ibid.*, 112.

appointed Professor H. Claude Horack.[92] This was a highly significant development. It was the beginning of an era of fact-finding on and material appraisal of legal education. Also, the appointment of Mr. Horack to the newly created position of Advisor was a wise one. He was then Secretary of the Association of American Law Schools and was thoroughly familiar with the hard facts of legal education. In his subsequent dealings with the personnel of the various law schools and with lawyers, he was sympathetic and helpful but firm. In December 1928 he was elected president of the Association of American Law Schools. He served as Advisor to the Council for over two years; he was then succeeded by Mr. Will Shafroth.

In 1929 William Draper Lewis was chairman of the Section. In his report that year to the Association he said that fourteen states were complying with the standards.[93] On January 1, 1930, Mr. Shafroth was appointed Advisor to the Council of the Section.[94] The progress made in legal education during the next decade was, in a substantial measure, attributable to his industry and vision. In 1931 the Chairman of the Section reported to the Association that under the leadership of the Section a national conference of bar examiners had been organized.[95] This was a highly salutary move. We have in the course of this study previously emphasized the sensitivity on matters relating to legal education of the profession, the schools, and the various boards of bar examiners, each to the actions and attitudes of the others. With the organization of the bar examiners of the various states into an association, three national agencies—the American Bar Association working through its Section of Legal Education and Admissions to

[92] *Ibid.*, 547.

[93] 54 Rep. Am. Bar Ass'n, 57 (1929).

[94] 55 Rep. Am. Bar Ass'n, 32 (1930).

[95] 56 Rep. Am. Bar Ass'n, 31 (1931).

the Bar, the Association of American Law Schools, and the National Conference of Bar Examiners—were at long last in operation. In the ensuing years the National Conference under the able directorship of Miss Marjorie Merritt has made a distinct place for itself in the field of legal education and admissions to the bar through the services it has rendered on and the direction it has given to matters of bar admission. Eight years after the organization of the National Conference, Mr. Robert G. Storey, then Chairman of the Section, paid tribute to it. The Conference, said he,[96]

> "has assumed an important place in the bar admission field and has been responsible for notable improvements in bar examination technique. Through a monthly journal it has kept the examiners aware of developments which are taking place in respect to admission requirements as well as the examinations themselves, and it is also working for the improvement of the character of applicants for admission and methods of character examination."

In his statement Mr. Storey commented on the progress of the program of continuing legal education for lawyers.[97] In 1937 the House of Delegates of the American Bar Association had directed the Association to sponsor and encourage a "nation wide program of post admission legal education for the benefit of the legal profession."[98] He went into detail on the number of institutes that had been conducted and the reception these courses had had from the members of the profession. This development, while it was initiated before World War II, did not become nationwide until after the War. Today, it is a vital meaning-

[96] 64 Rep. Am. Bar Ass'n, 452, 454 (1939).

[97] *Ibid.*, 456–462.

[98] 62 Rep. Am. Bar Ass'n, 964 (1937).

ful instrument of education for the members of the practicing bar.

The impact of the standards of legal education of the American Bar Association on bar admission requirements in the various states, and on the content and substance of the educational programs of the law schools, was marked and particularly so after the employment of a full-time adviser by the Council of the Section. In 1931 the Council reported to the Association that seventeen states were then requiring, either presently or prospectively, all applicants to have had two years of college work or its equivalent as a condition for admission to the bar.[99] The report that year showed that a total of 180 law schools were in operation in the United States and that 77 were approved; 98 were part-time, of which seven were approved.[100] In 1939 the Section reported that 41 states, containing over 90 percent of the entire number of law-school students of the country, then required two years of college work or its equivalent before admission to the bar.[101] One hundred and one from a total of 185 law schools were by that time on the approved list of the American Bar Association.[102] In 1951, from a total of 164 schools, 124 were approved. Forty were unapproved.[103] The report for 1951 showed a total enrollment in all law schools of 47,610 students. Of that number, 39,626 were enrolled in approved, and 7,984 in unapproved schools.[104] In 1950, 107 schools were members of the Association of American Law Schools.[105]

---

99 56 Rep. Am. Bar Ass'n, 609 (1931).

100 *Ibid.*, 611.

101 64 Rep. Am. Bar Ass'n, 452 (1939).

102 *Ibid.*, 454.

103 *Law Schools and Bar Admission Requirements*, 1951 Review of Legal Education, pamph. 5–17.

104 *Ibid.*, 18.

105 Handbook, Ass'n Am. L. Schools, 228–230 (1950).

In 1950 the American Bar Association amended its standard on prelegal education. On the motion of Mr. Richard Bentley, Chairman of the Section of Legal Education and Admissions to the Bar, the House of Delegates, at its midyear meeting, adopted a resolution, to become effective in the fall of 1952, that the standard for an approved law school be amended to read as follows:[106]

> "It shall require as a condition to admission at least three years of acceptable college work, except that a school which requires four years of full time work or an equivalent of part time work for the first professional degree in law may admit a student who has successfully completed two years of acceptable college work."

The following December the Association of American Law Schools adopted a similar resolution but approved it as a standard and not as a requirement.[107]

The criteria by which progress in legal education should be appraised may raise a debatable question. If it is to be measured by the yardstick of the standards of the American Bar Association and the Articles of the Association of American Law Schools, then it seems fair to conclude that, over the span of the years, the most substantial improvement has been made since the beginning of the present century. Each of these Associations has had its sphere of influence, but that of the American Bar Association has been broader and its programs have been more effectual,

---

[106] 75 Rep. Am. Bar Ass'n, 411–412 (1950).

[107] Handbook, Ass'n Am. L. Schools, 64–99 (1950). The Constitution of the Association of American Law Schools makes a distinction between "standards" and "requirements." Distinguished from constitutional requirements, the standards of the Association, as defined by President Llewellyn when the issue on this amendment was under debate, "have been things which we have in all respects viewed as desirable goals." *Ibid.*, 80.

particularly in their impact on the weaker law schools and on bar admission agencies. In the advancement of the standards of bar admission, the law school Association has played a minor if not a negligible role. The pressures it has brought to bear in the advancement of the cause of legal education have, in the main, been on the law schools. It should be emphasized that it is an association of schools, and that from the time of its organization it has operated under a set of standards that all schools had to comply with as a condition to membership in the group. Further, it created a forum conceived to promote discussion and action on questions of legal education. And so by gradual steps, through the discussions it stimulated, the horizons of teachers on matters of legal education were extended, and through legislative action by the Association the more timid and backward member schools were forced to improve their facilities for and their programs of education. Through the measures it has sponsored and promoted, the Association has indeed been a potent agency for the improvement of the quality of the work done in member schools, and this in turn has tended to advance the cause of legal education generally.

M. THE AMERICAN LAW INSTITUTE

We must not take it that the Association of American Law Schools has worked exclusively within a limited orbit. One of the great professional organizations of our day is the American Law Institute, and the germ of the idea of the Institute was planted in 1914 by Professor Wesley N. Hohfeld in an address, "A Vital School of Jurisprudence and Law," delivered before the law school Association.[108] The following year the President of the Association, Harry S. Richards, in his address, referred to Hohfeld's paper.[109]

108 Handbook, Ass'n Am. L. Schools, 76 (1914).
109 Handbook, Ass'n Am. L. Schools, 75–76 (1915).

Growing out of the discussion on the President's address a committee was authorized to consider, among other things, a center of the sort envisioned by Hohfeld.[110] At the conclusion of the 1915 session the President announced the appointment of a "Committee on the Feasibility of Establishing a Center for the Study of Comparative Law and Jurisprudence."[111] This committee later became known as the Committee on the Juristic Center. After several years devoted to the incubation of the idea, the Committee on the Juristic Center, then under the chairmanship of Joseph H. Beale, reported to the Association in 1922 that it had invited a group of men "representing all branches of the profession" to meet with it in New York in May 1922; that those who attended had constituted themselves a Committee on the Establishment of a Permanent Organization for the Improvement of the Law; and that this new committee had then proceeded to elect officers as follows: Elihu Root, President; George W. Wickersham, Vice-President; William Draper Lewis, Executive Secretary; and George W. Murray, Treasurer. Professor Beale's committee also reported that on May 24, 1922, the Carnegie Corporation had granted the newly created committee the sum of $25,000 for the prosecution of its work.[112] In 1923, Beale reported to the Association: "The Committee on the Juristic Center begs leave to report that on February 23rd, 1923, the Committee on the Establishment of a Permanent Organization for Improvement of the Law, into which this Committee had been merged, convened a meeting of all branches of the legal profession in Washington, D. C., and at that meeting the American Law Institute was formed."[113]

---

110 *Ibid.*, 27–28.

111 *Ibid.*, 59.

112 Handbook, Ass'n Am. L. Schools, 37–38 (1922).

113 Handbook, Ass'n Am. L. Schools, 37 (1923). A complete account of the work of the Institute is given by Judge Goodrich in his

N. IN PERSPECTIVE

In perspective, the American Bar Association and the Association of American Law Schools have been and are mighty forces for the advancement of legal education. We are apt to fret over the tardiness with which improvement comes about, but viewed over the long reach of the years, it is clear that much progress has been made, and it is equally clear that the tempo of progress was materially accelerated when those two great protagonists entered the arena of legal education. Even so, major problems remain and one of them is the unapproved law school. The Association of American Law Schools is unable to solve this problem, if for no other reason, because of the nature of its organization. It is an association of schools. A school must seek admission to membership in it. If a law school is satisfied to remain outside the orbit of this group, there is little or nothing that the Association can do about that school. The program of the American Bar Association is broader and has been effective in mitigating the disruptive implications of the unapproved school. Through its work with bar admission authorities and the bar in the several states; through its inspections of the law schools; and particularly through the publication of lists of approved and unapproved schools, the number of inferior schools has, in the last twenty-five years, been materially reduced. Notwithstanding, forty law schools not approved by the American Bar Association are in operation in the United States. A national agency cannot force the issue, and this highlights both the strength and weakness of the American system of government. On bar admission the states are supreme. The American Bar Association has accomplished much through persuasion and through indirect pressures,

---

report to the Survey of the Legal Profession, Goodrich, *The Story of the American Law Institute*, 1951 Wash. U. L. Q. 283.

but the onus for bringing about material improvements in legal education and admission to the bar in the several states must ultimately fall on the lawyers of those states.

Another observation is pertinent. The standards of the American Bar Association and the requirements of the Association of American Law Schools, which in fact closely parallel each other, deal primarily with measures of quantity—so many years of prelegal study, so many of law study, a specified number of books in a law-school library, a minimum number of full-time teachers in each school, etc. These, indeed, are factors that should not be disparaged as measures of merit, but in themselves they do not go to the substance of things. When improvements in legal education were first pressed, they probably were the only yardsticks that could have been employed. But are we not now ready for the introduction of a new and better standard of measurement—one that stresses quality? Professor Sullivan in his admirable study concluded it with the statement that the emphasis in the future should be "on the quality of legal education."[114] Specifically, this means stressing the quality of the content of the educational programs of the schools, and the quality, both of mind and of character, of the individuals admitted to the bar. The content of an educational program is primarily the responsibility of the schools. The establishment of standards for admission to the bar has broader implications as to responsibility. Assurance against the admission of unqualified persons to the bar is a matter of grave public concern. But the public as such does not have the discernment for setting up measures for its own protection. Responsibility for these measures must rest on the schools, the bar examiners, the courts, and ultimately on the profession.

---

[114] *The Professional Associations and Legal Education,* 4 J. Legal Ed. 401, 426 (1952).

VII. CRITICISMS OF MODERN LEGAL EDUCATION

An appraisal of the criticisms of legal education is a sensitive task. It calls for judgments in an area where opinions vary widely. First, we must determine what the criticisms are and distinguish valid contentions from those that are mere shots in the dark. Another problem is one of evaluation—of assessing the relative force of the arguments that have been made. The task is further complicated because the critics all too often fail to define the premises on which they base their contentions. What is their standard of judgment? This raises a question on the objectives of legal education. What is legal education trying, or what should it be trying to accomplish? The latter question is fundamental and should be answered before any attempt is made to say wherein education has failed. But to attempt to answer this question is a hazardous undertaking.

A. The Objectives of Legal Education

The statement is frequently made that the object of legal education is to train individuals to be good lawyers. "In the last analysis," said the Board that made the study on legal education in California in 1949,[1] "legal education has two related objectives—the training of lawyers, and the improvement of the law. The latter objective in particular requires not merely that poor law schools be eliminated, but that the best law schools be made better." This is a true statement and one with which most if not all critics will agree. Obviously, though, it does not come to grips with the pertinent question as to what is an educational

[1] Legal Education and Admissions to the Bar in California, 139 (1949). This study was made by Joseph A. McClain, Jr., Thomas F. McDonald and Sidney Post Simpson.

program that will produce these results—as to what the content of the program should be, its method of instruction, its administration. A statement on this subject by a committee of the Harvard Law School staff varies in emphasis from the California one, but not in substance. "A university law school has two purposes," said that committee,[2] "(1) to train men for the legal profession; (2) to provide a center where scholars may contribute to an understanding of law and government and may participate creatively in their growth and improvement." A later statement in the Harvard study comes closer to the point of immediate inquiry. "An outstanding quality of the successful lawyer," observed the Committee,[3] "is his capacity for adaptation to new tasks and his ability to educate himself to meet constantly changing demands."

Dean Cecil A. Wright of the School of Law of the University of Toronto, in a very able discussion, has suggested that "the three big objectives of a university law school" should be: "(1) education in the *qualities* that should be found in a legal practitioner; (2) education that will train a man not merely in the work of solving problems of individual clients but of the society in which he lives; and (3) to act as a centre of research, criticism, and contribution to the better understanding of the laws by which societies are held together."[4] Professor W. Barton Leach has given us a job analysis. "The men whom we are now training," said he,[5] "must be prepared to perform two

[2] Preliminary Statement of the Committee on Legal Education of the Harvard Law School, 4 (1947).

[3] *Ibid.*, 6.

[4] *The University Law Schools*, 2 J. Legal Ed. 409, 412 (1950). Another good analysis has been made by Mr. Chief Justice Arthur T. Vanderbilt: *The Responsibilities of Our Law Schools to the Public and the Profession*, 3 J. Legal Ed. 207 (1950).

[5] *Property Law Taught in Two Packages*, 1 J. Legal Ed. 28, 29 (1948).

tasks during the productive years of their professional lives:

"1. *To assume direction of all phases of the areas of personal conflict inherent in a complex society and economy.* They must be advisers, negotiators, advocates, judges, arbitrators—and frequently administrators and executives having a large amount of quasi-legislative power . . .

"2. *To provide a very large proportion of national leadership at all levels of authority.*"

What are the implications of the foregoing statements for legal education? We start from the premise that the work of no other profession, no other calling, requires of its votaries so high a degree of versatility, insight, and imagination as is demanded of lawyers. Knowledge is a factor—knowledge over a wide range of subjects, legal and non-legal. Aptitudes and skills are involved. The lawyer is a craftsman and the aim of legal education must be to inculcate in him the skills of the craft. But the lawyer must be much more than a good craftsman. Professor Leach has listed the following as the basic qualities of a good lawyer: fact consciousness; a sense of relevance; comprehensiveness; foresight; lingual sophistication; precision and persuasiveness of speech; "and finally, and pervading all the rest, and possibly the only one that is really basic: *self-discipline in habits of thoroughness,* an abhorrence of superficiality and approximation."[6]

It would be too much to assume that legal education, meaning here *law-school* education, can fully endow students with these qualities. The education of a lawyer is a lifetime undertaking. It should, however, be the aim of a law

[6] *Ibid.*, 30–31. No study of the subject under consideration is complete without the reading of the excellent report of the Committee on Curriculum, Handbook, Ass'n Am. L. Schools, 159 (1944), and Vanderbilt, *A Report on Prelegal Education,* 25 N. Y. U. L. Rev. 199 (1950).

school to plant in the minds of its students the seeds of these qualities and to nurture their growth. May we envision here the qualities mentioned by Professor Leach and another one: a quality more intangible but of the essence. It involves an attitude of mind—a mind that can think, as successive problems arise for solution, untrammeled by preconceptions. The lawyer, if he is to meet the complex demands which modern society makes on him, must have a deep sense of social responsibility and he must be highly versatile, versatile in the sense of having an aptitude for new tasks. The "discipline we should seek in law school," as Professor Lon L. Fuller has described it,[7] "is that which sets the student's mind free, not that which makes it comfortable within a framework imposed on it from outside." These are high and perhaps idealistic goals for legal education. Obviously, the measure of their attainment must depend substantially on the quality of the individuals admitted to law study—their abilities, aptitudes and character—and upon the caliber of the men who teach them.

In the light of this listing of objectives, what is the present situation as to legal education, and what are the principal criticisms of it? Most of the criticisms that have been made are directed at the professional curriculum, but before dealing with them, may we first record some general observations that relate to (1) the unapproved law school, (2) prelegal education, and (3) the general financial status of law schools.

B. THE UNAPPROVED LAW SCHOOL

The unapproved school is the maverick of legal education. We have already paid our respects to it. The argument has been made that some approved schools are no better than, if as good as, some that are unapproved. That may be

[7] *On Teaching Law*, 3 Stanford L. Rev. 35, 38 (1950).

true. The standards bearing on approved schools are not exacting, and, as we have seen, are wanting in criteria bearing on quality—quality of content of the curriculum, of the work done, and of the students who are admitted to law study. But the approved schools have met the tests of a standardizing agency, and they are subject to the promptings of that agency for further improvement. It is possible that the American Bar Association could bring yet greater pressures on the unapproved schools than it does, but so long as some states permit these schools to exist, and so long as these states will, in their respective jurisdictions, make applicants who have pursued work in these schools eligible for bar examinations, the problem of the unapproved schools will persist. And it is equally clear that while these schools remain on the scene, they will continue to be a demoralizing factor to legal education. On the favorable side of this issue, we note the fact that much progress has been made, particularly in the last thirty years, toward the solution of this problem.

C. PRELEGAL EDUCATION

The subject of prelegal education has been fully covered in an excellent study prepared for the Survey of the Legal Profession by Mr. Chief Justice Arthur T. Vanderbilt.[8] I have previously touched on it under the heading, *Impact of Professional Organizations.* A brief excursion into this field at this point is also indicated, for, of all the criticisms of legal education, that directed against prelegal education is one of the most articulate. Legal education, as I have heretofore stressed, is a lifetime undertaking. It should be viewed not in piecemeal but as a synthesis. The law schools have centered their efforts on that phase of legal

[8] *A Report on Prelegal Education,* 25 N. Y. U. L. Rev. 199 (1950). Also an earlier study by Vanderbilt, A Report on Prelegal Education, pamph. (1944).

education that is confined to the years the student spends in law school. They have been shortsighted, however, if not neglectful of their responsibilities, in focusing their attention exclusively on that area. Many of the problems of legal education owe their being to deficiencies in the prelegal period. What we are dealing with here is a problem of perspective. I venture the thesis that law teachers are unable to get an adequate perspective on their immediate assignments unless they have an insight into what use their students have made of their time before entering law school. While the problem of prelegal education is a broad one and the inquiry might be extended into the student's background even before college, we are directing these remarks to the college work the student takes before beginning his law studies—the span of three or four years of study in college which should be very meaningful in its bearing later on the student's success in law school and still later on his success in the practice. On this important problem the law schools have offered little or nothing of guidance. The subject has been discussed by law teachers, but, as Judge Vanderbilt has shown, these discussions have yielded nothing that is concrete. Some teachers, indeed, have taken the position that this subject is none of their business.[9]

Broadly speaking, the evolution of Anglo-American legal education has been characterized by three methods of approach: that typified by the severely practical method of the apprenticeship system; that which stressed a broad course of instruction and which found expression in Blackstone's first lecture and later in the programs projected

[9] Handbook, Ass'n Am. L. Schools, 112 (1930), and particularly the remarks by Professor Beale. A promising approach to the subject of prelegal education is being made by the present Committee on Pre-Legal Education of the Association of American Law Schools. That Committee has recently published a "draft of a policy statement." *On the Aims and Quality of Pre-Legal Education: An Association View?* 4 J. Legal Ed. 441 (1952).

in the early post-Revolutionary era by the apostles of legal education in America; and that which was initiated by Story and later amplified and dramatized through the introduction of the case method by Langdell, which substantially isolated the study of law from its social environment. The first of these trends, apprenticeship training as an exclusive method of legal education, is disappearing, though the problem of instruction in the practical skills of the profession remains.

The second approach, which emphasized a broadly synthesized course of instruction, has never lost its appeal to discerning members of the profession. Its acceptance as the underlying principle of the law-school curriculum remains today a major issue in legal education. The pioneers of education who sponsored it were unable to carry their ideas to fulfillment, but, as we have seen, their views through the years have had the support of many leaders of the profession. After Blackstone's famous crusade in England, his views came to the forefront again in the mid-1800's, this time under the sponsorship of Lord Westbury (Richard Bethell). From the early period of Lord Westbury's career in Parliament, he was persistent, Atlay has related,[10] in his

> "advocacy of the cause of legal education. Not only had the teaching of law fallen into utter desuetude at Oxford and Cambridge, but the Inns of Court were only slowly awakening to their responsibilities. Some years previously he had drawn the attention of these latter bodies to their neglected duty, and it was due in no small measure to his efforts that lectures and readerships and studentships were gradually established; that the Council of Legal Education, of which he was one of the earliest presidents, was called into existence; and that examina-

[10] 2 The Victorian Chancellors, 232–233 (1908).

> tions were made compulsory upon all who sought to be called to the Bar. But Bethell's ideals soared much higher than this, to the creation of a great legal university in London which might impart that instruction in original principles the want of which has been the perennial reproach of the English Bar and is largely responsible for the haphazard and misdirected growth of so many branches of our law."

In our time, and in the United States, where progress on this subject is recorded, Mr. Chief Justice Vanderbilt nevertheless found cause to express concern over it. "It is singular," said he,[11] "that in an age when it is manifest that broad enlightened leadership is essential to the survival of civilization there should be anything less than a unanimous vote as to the necessity of the widest possible training for our public leaders."

The method and materials involved in the third approach to legal education became a pattern for the prevailing system in the United States. As projected by Langdell, printed books were the *ultimate sources of all legal knowledge* and the content of these printed books was to be made up of selected cases—selected decisions of appellate courts. Thus, students were confined in their study of the law to the reading of adjudicated cases. The view came to be that the law is self-sufficient, and that neither the law student nor the lawyer had need to look beyond the adjudicated cases for the materials of the law. The demand for a broader training, however, could not be denied. The solution evolved was to specify a period of prelaw study which as we have seen has, under the standards of the American Bar Association, recently been increased to a minimum of three years of college work. Apparently, judging by the

[11] *A Report on Prelegal Education,* 25 N. Y. U. L. Rev. 199, 211 (1950).

silence of the standards on this point, the content of the prelegal program is unimportant. What matters is that the applicant for law study has accumulated credit over a period of three years of college work.[12]

What does all this add up to as a program of legal education? Broadly viewed, it involves three years of college work stipulated as a prerequisite for admission to a law school, this followed by three years of law study. The Standards of the Association of American Law Schools state that the work taken must have been in courses with "substantive content or training," but no guidance is proferred the student as to those courses that might give him perspective on his responsibilities as a lawyer and as a citizen. Nothing is said about courses that might prepare him for the skills of the profession. Prelegal and legal education are in fact divorced from each other, or if not that, exist under an agreement of separate maintenance. There is no attempt at synthesis, and no cognizance is taken of the broad concept entertained by the American pioneers of legal education. The student is left to his own devices in the selection of his prelegal work. Anyone familiar with the huge offerings of fragmentized courses of a university must realize that the student is likely to come through this ordeal with an education that is little more than a patchwork.

We must not overstate this situation. There is value in college work as such. Also, if the student chooses his instructors wisely, he may come into contact with some stimulating minds. Communion with great teachers, re-

[12] Sec. VI–1A of the Standards of the Association of American Law Schools provides: "Beginning in the fall of 1952, a member school and a school to be acceptable for membership shall require at least three years of acceptable college work for the admission of students." In Sec. VI–3 "acceptable credit" is defined as "credit earned in courses with substantive content or training."

gardless of subject matter, is an educational experience. But the rub is that the requirement—a minimum of three years of college work—leaves all this to chance. Neither the authority that established the requirement, nor the schools, excepting in the sporadic actions of some schools, offer the student guidance on the path he should follow. Why, as a measure of educational policy, does he not have that guidance? The answer is made that neither law teachers nor lawyers can agree on the content of his college course. But that answer tends to weaken the basic assumptions underlying the requirement. Occasionally law teachers have expressed a lack of confidence in college work, but if this distrust has merit, it further weakens the case for the requirement. The law schools do, indeed, deplore the substance of the college work which students have taken. The most vocal complaint is that they are deficient in English. A number of schools have, in fact, sought to remedy that deficiency through inserting courses in legal writing into their law programs. But why take up the precious time of the law-school period to correct a defect that ought to have been corrected before the student entered law school? Surely, every law teacher, every lawyer will agree that a reasonable mastery of the English language is a prime qualification of the law student and of the lawyer. If that be true, then why not do something about it? Even if we assume that the schools cannot agree on the full content of a prelaw program, does it follow that they cannot agree on some courses, starting with English, that the student should take and in which he should show proficiency as a condition to being admitted to law study? With agreement on English, perhaps other accords can be reached. "It may be pertinent to remark," observed Judge Vanderbilt,[13]

[13] *A Report on Prelegal Education,* 25 N. Y. U. L. Rev. 199, 216 (1950).

"that in the field of strict prelegal training it is the social sciences (history, government, economics, sociology) and to a less degree the physical and biological sciences that may reveal the 'is' of the social order, as ethics and philosophy may disclose the 'ought.' This we must continuously compare with the 'must, or else' of the law in an effort to draw the three together, while we must look to psychology, logic and the methods of science to guide the reason that plays so large a part in the field of law. Yet in the same breath we must admit that more insight and inspiration may often be found in a minute of poetry or drama than in any hour of science or philosophy. The problem is one that calls for the deliberations of the ablest men from the colleges and from among those interested in legal education."

The question is, however, broader than that of setting up requirements as to prelaw courses. Beyond the benefits that might be gained through the prescription of some courses, and particularly prescription of courses on skill-training, there remains the basic question of synthesis and fusion. One problem is, as Dean Wright has pointed out,[14] that students on reaching the law school seldom are able to relate the work they had in their prelaw course to that in the law school. "There is little reason to think," commented the Harvard Committee, "that any substantial contribution can be made to the problem of a fusion of the social sciences merely by prescribing the prelegal course of study." Accordingly, there has been, the Committee went on to say, "an increasing tendency in American law schools to make it possible for law students to study such subjects as economics and psychology after they have completed

[14] *The University Law Schools*, 2 J. Legal Ed. 409, 418 (1950).

the elementary law courses."[15] This is a development of great promise. It was a basic factor in the setting up of four-year programs by some law schools. Unfortunately, however, a few of the schools that adopted that program used it merely as a vehicle for packing more orthodox law courses into it. Also, the fact is to be noted that an increasing number of law teachers are today fusing legal and relevant non-legal materials in the teaching of their law courses. Perspective in law teaching has, indeed, changed materially since the days when law was conceived to be a science, all the materials of which were restricted to selected appellate court decisions. Even so, the winning of optimal educational advantages for the student from his prelegal course, and the synthesis of legal and non-legal materials and ideas in relation thereto are among the foremost problems in legal education today.

D. THE FINANCIAL STATUS OF LAW SCHOOLS

Another broad observation about legal education is that it is not adequately financed. The historic reasons for this are apparent. Apprenticeship training was cheap. The transition from the apprentice system to lecture schools, conducted by practitioners, was a natural one, but here again little expense was involved. All that these schools required was a lecturer, a few students, a room for the class, and, perhaps, a few books. The lawyer-lecturer was primarily a practitioner who gave but a limited amount of his time to his students. All this is, of course, changed now, though some so-called schools of this sort still exist. The fact is, however, that legal education has never been able to dispel the widespread impression that it provides a relatively inexpensive type of instruction. Through the years many

[15] Preliminary Statement of the Committee on Legal Education of the Harvard Law School, 111 (1947).

law schools, both non-university and university, have been supported primarily, or wholly, from student fees. Not only is this true, but some university administrations have actually made it a practice to draw on the student-fee income of their law schools to help support other divisions of their institutions. Esther Lucile Brown, in a study sponsored by the Russell Sage Foundation, has commented critically on this situation. "At the earliest possible moment," said she,[16]

> "a thorough, completely objective study of the existent financial situation in legal education ought to be made. . . . The study should be immediately followed by an educational program designed to make known, not only to the entire bar and bench but to all interested laity, exactly what is being paid for legal education, what can be provided for that sum, and what is requisite for a type of professional education that will fit men with the maximum of efficiency for the essential functions not only of legal craftsman but of policy-maker and administrator."

The problem was pungently phrased in the California study. "The law schools in California," commented the Board that made the survey,[17]

> "in common with law schools throughout the United States, are suffering from financial starvation, and have been from the time of their organization. Vast sums of money have been made available for education and research in medicine and in various scientific fields, but practically none has been provided for the education of the bar or research into those problems of social and legal engineering with which the legal profession has a public duty to deal."

[16] Lawyers, Law Schools and the Public Service, 251–252 (1948).

[17] Legal Education and Admissions to the Bar in California, 74 (1949).

Recently, in an illuminating address, Dean Griswold also touched on this subject.[18] He spoke of research in the area of human relations, involving the broad context of the social sciences and law. He emphasized that the problems in this field are vastly more complex than those in the natural sciences. And, we add parenthetically, and with no intent to disparage the excellent research carried on in other fields, the need for research in the area of human relations is greater than in the sciences; it is imperative. One thing that will, however, have to be understood, stressed Dean Griswold,[19]

> "is that this task will require large sums of money. There is little conception yet of the inevitable high costs of research in this field. . . . We think little of putting $10,000,000 or more into a cyclotron, while my school has for years had extreme difficulty in raising $25,000 a year to cover the costs of a remarkable and productive basic research into the causes of juvenile delinquency and the effectiveness of present methods of dealing with that vastly important problem."

What are the implications of this situation? It discloses, first of all, a lack of aggressiveness and perhaps of imagination on the part of the profession and on the part of the law schools in the advancement of the cause of legal education. The context of the ideas with which the lawyer and the law teacher have worked has had a limited circumference. Our ideas on law have been held captive by tradition and environment. In accordance with our English heritage, the attention of the profession has been focused on the common law. The apostles of legal education in America sought to transcend those restrictions by projecting a broadly synthesized program of legal education. Their plans came to

[18] *Educating Lawyers for a Changing World: A Challenge to Our Law Schools*, 37 A.B.A. Jour. 805 (1951).

[19] *Ibid.*, 808.

grief in the stagnant waters of indifference. And while, as we have seen, their views through the years have persisted, they were checked in their fulfillment by a virile movement in legal education—the case method of instruction. With the triumph of the case method, legal education accepted the tenet that law was self-contained. And so long as legal education is confined to the study and the teaching of cases, it will be an inexpensive affair. Further, so long as legal research is restricted to the study and analysis of cases, it, too, with full tribute to the magnificent work done by great legal scholars, will be relatively inexpensive. There is no virtue in costly education and research merely for the sake of cost. The object is to establish the best possible program of legal education and research and if that should require more extensive financing, then funds should be found for it. A fusion of legal and non-legal disciplines into a broad program of legal education, as we have contemplated, would require better financing. And if the schools were to launch into new areas of research, as indicated by Dean Griswold, much greater sums of money would be required. We are envisioning here a program of research that touches not only scholarly treatises and analytical articles dealing with court decisions and legislation—this work, to be sure, must go on—but of research into the basic factors of human behavior. The law does not operate *in vacuo.* It is an instrument set up by society for the solution of human problems. What are those problems? What is it that gives rise to them? What is the key to their solution? Here lies the field of labor, a vast and inviting area of research. This type of research is potentially of much greater significance to human welfare than anything that has been done in the physical sciences. But this type of research is costly.

E. CRITICISMS OF THE CASE METHOD

The criticisms of the professional programs of the law schools are difficult to classify since they shade into one another and as a consequence vary from each other only in emphasis. Broadly, all can be grouped under one heading, that the schools do not adequately prepare students for the tasks they will have to perform in the practice. More specifically they relate to the following: (1) that the programs of instruction, with their emphasis on case study, are time-consuming, without commensurate educational returns to the students; (2) that they are lacking in perspective as to the scope and implications of the law, and as to the problems the lawyer must solve in the practice; (3) that they fail to provide a synthesis of the law and a synthesis of law and related disciplines; (4) that they neglect training in the practical skills a lawyer must have; and (5) that they fail to inculcate in students an understanding of professional standards and ideals.

Case instruction, which since the time of Langdell has been the bone and sinew of American legal education, draws the weight of the criticisms. But this statement requires clarification. There is general agreement among law teachers and substantial agreement among the members of the bar that case study is an indispensable phase of legal education. "The tremendous vitality of American legal education," said the Harvard Committee,[20]

> "exists because it focuses instruction on cases and problems instead of abstract theories. The skilful editor of a casebook purposely throws cases into a juxtaposition that provokes the student to intellectual activity. The student is challenged to reconcile discrepancies, to explain conflicts, to pick up the tangled threads of thought

[20] Preliminary Statement of the Committee on Legal Education of the Harvard Law School, 115 (1947).

> where they are left by the decisions and put them in order. There are few who do not respond to this stimulus."

"Case-instruction," commented the Association of American Law Schools' Committee on Curriculum,[21]

> "is not only the most significant American contribution to legal education, but it is unrivaled as a machinery for basic training in analysis of holdings and in application of doctrine. It is amazingly flexible. It can be readily adjusted to almost any size of class and almost any instructor's individuality. It is certainly a necessary part of future American legal education."

These are valid appraisals of the case system. The case method is a telling medium of teaching in the hands of any competent instructor, and in the hands of a gifted teacher it is a superb device. "You can do anything," said Wendell Phillips, "with a bayonet—except sit upon it."[22] A talented law teacher can do almost everything essential to a legal education with case instruction. The evangelistic fervor over the case method that characterized Langdell's early disciples is not found in law teachers of the present day, but this does not detract from the fact that case study is a most effective instrument of education. The criticisms of it are not directed at its intrinsic merits, but against making case study and case teaching the sole content of legal education.

What is becoming apparent now is that the overwhelming success of method in case study distracted attention from its educational limitations. One of these limitations is the fact that after the first year of law study, there is a distinct lag of interest in the reading of cases on the part of law

[21] *Committee on Curriculum*, Handbook, Ass'n Am. L. Schools, 159, 166 (1944).

[22] Quoted, 5 Wigmore on Evidence, 29 (3d ed. 1940).

students. The method by that time has lost much of its sparkle. This was noted by the Committee of the Association of American Law Schools from whose report we have just quoted. Case instruction, observed the Committee,[23]

> "is an almost unique machinery to aid an instructor of average gifts to both organize his instruction and hold the attention and interest of his class. This virtue begins to fade, at present, by the second semester. On the attention and interest side the virtue is at present almost absent by the fifth or sixth semester. There it now takes instructor's skill, variation and addition, or else peculiarly interesting material, to make case-instruction go over to satisfaction; it ceases to be the method which carries the instructor and becomes instead a question of the instructor carrying the method."

There are differences of opinion as to when the interest in case study begins to fade and differences as to the extent to which it declines, but the general tenor of the Committee's observation is correct. We are dealing here with an educational phenomenon which gives rise to a valid criticism of legal education and one with which the law schools must reckon.

Case study is time-consuming. Law teachers have been sensitive to this factor ever since the introduction of the case method. They were reconciled to it, however, in the belief that the educational value of case study was so positive that it negated all other considerations. Apparently they gave no serious consideration to the diminishing-returns factor. Now, if it be true that there is a distinct fading of interest in the reading of cases after the student's first year in law school, then the argument that case study takes an undue amount of time becomes a formidable one.

[23] Supra, note 21, p. 166.

This view has been emphasized by Llewellyn. "In any event," he observed,[24]

> "three things are obvious. The first is that the skills properly to be derived from case teaching are essential to every lawyer. The second is that the handling of all or the bulk of the inculcation of the rules of law by way of the case-class (which comes, before the third year, to deaden students' interest as much as in the first semester it stimulated that interest) is so costly in time as to make the amount of information acquired about the more important or typical fields of law definitely inadequate for any graduate. The third thing is that along with the so-called 'case skills' there are many other craft-skills of the lawyer which the schools can and should impart both in theory and in practice."

F. LACK OF PERSPECTIVE

A broad criticism, and one of substantial merit, of the law schools is that their programs of instruction are lacking in breadth and perspective, and that they are not keyed to the problems lawyers must solve in the practice. Here, varying only in emphasis, we are wrestling once more with the question of broad outlook on the tasks of the lawyer with which the pioneers of legal education in America were concerned. The profession is a dynamic force in society. Because of its strategic position, the public does and necessarily must look to the profession for guidance and leadership. What is more, in an era of economic and social change, new skills and new talents are constantly demanded of lawyers. The lawyer is no longer primarily an advocate; gone are the

[24] *The Current Crisis in Legal Education*, 1 J. Legal Ed. 211, 216 (1948). Llewellyn was chairman of the Committee on Curriculum of the Association of American Law Schools which wrote the 1944 Report.

days of the resonant phrases of the orator. Only a relative few of the profession now devote themselves to court procedure and the trial of cases. The lawyer today is a counselor, draftsman, negotiator, and planner. In the complicated economic and social structure of our time, with its cross-currents produced by an overlapping of interests, it is the lawyer's forte to be guide and legislator in the solution of these problems. Lest this be interpreted as touching only those phases of a lawyer's work which relate to big enterprise, may we point out that skills and talents of this sort are demanded of the lawyer in work on much simpler levels. The time was, when a client wished a will drawn, he made his desires known to his lawyer who thereupon proceeded to draft the will. The services performed by the lawyer were essentially those of a legal craftsman. Today's lawyer is an adviser to his client not only on legal matters but on related matters arising from other disciplines. Clearly, the lawyer now must be something of an economist, and the better economist he is, the better lawyer he is likely to be.

A law school that sets for itself only the routine assignment of teaching case law is not likely to develop an understanding of the changing currents in the work of the profession. Case law gives some indication, but it represents only a part of the field in which the lawyer must operate. "The profession itself," observed the Harvard Committee,[25]

> "expects something more of the School than that it should reflect inertly the practices and standards of today. . . . The School cannot train men adequately for a changing profession unless it is itself in the main stream of change, participating actively in its direction."

One of the neglected fields in legal education is that of

---

[25] Preliminary Statement of the Committee on Legal Education of the Harvard Law School, 6 (1947).

legislation. In using the term "legislation," I have in mind a broader connotation than that which includes the mere study of statutes. It involves proficiency in statutory law and much more. The legislative process, as Professor Fuller has said, presents the lawyer "as a planner, negotiator, and draftsman." Legislation refers not merely to the planning and drafting of statutes but

> "includes the negotiation and drafting of contracts and other private documents. Thus, the drafting of a will is, in this sense, legislation, since it establishes a legal framework within which the estate of the testator is administered after his death."[26]

It is passing strange that law teachers could at any time, at least in the modern era, have ignored a phase so real, so essential to the education of lawyers as the legislative process. It is an enigma that can be explained only in the light of the facts of history. Even so, any explanation must leave much to conjecture. Our English heritage with its strong emphasis on judge-made law no doubt was a contributing factor. With the introduction of the case method and the acceptance of Langdell's premise that printed books, consisting solely of reported cases, were the ultimate sources of a legal education, the mold that shaped the materials of legal education was fixed. Statutory law and related operations in the broader context of the legislative process, as Fuller has defined the term, were not in the mold, and it was not until the last twenty-five or thirty years that law teachers began seriously to question this arrangement. Later I shall wish to say something about recent developments in this area.

But the criticism touching the neglect of the legislative process is but a phase of the more comprehensive one aimed at the restricted scope of legal education. This criticism

---

[23] *What the Law Schools Can Contribute to the Making of Lawyers*, 1 J. Legal Ed. 189, 192–193 (1948).

attacks the assumption that law is a discipline that is self-contained and self-sufficient. Its premise is that the law pervades all phases of human activity and that it cannot be treated in isolation from related disciplines. "I cannot but believe," said Holmes in an address over a half-century ago,[27] "that if the training of lawyers led them habitually to consider more definitely and explicitly the social advantage on which the rule they lay down must be justified, they sometimes would hesitate where now they are confident, and see that really they were taking sides upon debatable and often burning questions." It was in this address that he in one sentence characterized legal education then current, and also pointed the way for its future development. "For the rational study of the law," said he,[28] "the black-letter man may be the man of the present, but the man of the future is the man of statistics and the master of economics."

This criticism, while directed generally at legal education, centers on the case method and is traceable, according to Hurst,[29]

> "to one radical defect. The case method isolated the study of law from the living context of the society. The student of law needed to be aware of the pressure of politics, the strands of class, religious, racial and national attitudes woven into the values and patterns of behavior with which law dealt; he needed some appreciation of the balance of power within the community, the clash of interests, and the contriving of economic institutions, as all these influenced and were influenced by the effort to order the society under law. But of all this, so far as the law school was concerned, the student was made aware only incidentally—as he glimpsed the social context through recitals of fact and appraisal, of

---

27 *The Path of the Law* in Collected Legal Papers, 167, 184 (1921).
28 *Ibid.*, 187.
29 The Growth of American Law, 265–266 (1950).

widely varying accuracy and imagination, in the reported opinions of appellate courts."

G. FAILURE TO PROVIDE SYNTHESIS

Another phase of the broad criticism that legal education is too restricted relates to the fact that the training given students emphasizes primarily the particulars of the law; that it fails to give them an historical grounding; and that it ignores the importance of studying law in the terms of universals. Stated more briefly, the criticism is that students are schooled to see the trees and not the forest. The concept that ruled case instruction, in its restricted use, was the antithesis of that entertained by the pioneers of legal education in the formative years of the Republic. Under the case method, observed Redlich,[30] a friendly critic,

> "legal education has assumed the form of instruction almost exclusively through analysis of separate cases. The result of this is that the students never obtain a general picture of the law as a whole, not even a picture which includes only its main features."

This criticism was pointedly stated by the Harvard Committee. "If a student knows anything of legal philosophy and its main currents," commented that Committee,[31]

> "it will be because he is one of the small number who take Jurisprudence because he has studied this subject outside the law school. . . . It has been said that the trouble with the present generation is that it has never read the minutes of the last meeting. Certainly it is paradoxical that the law schools, often accused of being too addicted to history, should so completely ig-

[30] The Case Method in American Law Schools, 41 (Carneg. Found. Bul. 8, 1914).

[31] Preliminary Statement of the Committee on Legal Education of the Harvard Law School, 127–128 (1947).

nore the major intellectual currents that have influenced the growth of the law in the past, particularly those that have shaped American legal and governmental institutions."

We are dealing with criticisms that have substance. What should the law schools do about them? One approach suggests itself. The standards of the American Bar Association now state that an approved law school must require a minimum of three years of prelegal work for admission, this to be followed by a minimum of three years of law study. We point out that one of the major problems of legal education centers in the use the student makes of his time during the prelegal period, and in the coordination and synthesis of his prelegal and legal studies. The current Committee on Pre-Legal Education of the Association of American Law Schools has made a keen appraisal of the situation. "Every passing year," said that Committee,[32]

> "makes increasingly evident the vital concern which law schools necessarily have with the quality of the preparation incoming students bring with them from their undergraduate years. For unless that preparation has been of high quality, the law schools cannot, in the additional time which they can fairly require of their students, equip them for satisfactory performance within the legal profession and the democratic community."

These are encouraging words. The quality of prelegal preparation is a matter of prime importance. We express the hope that the Committee will go further and point the way for the schools to bring about that improvement. And beyond that, there looms yet another, and perhaps an even more significant question which relates to the coordination and synthesis of prelegal and legal studies.

32 *On the Aims and Quality of Pre-Legal Education: An Association View?* 4 J. Legal Ed. 441, 442 (1952).

The extent to which the case method should be employed in the law schools is another question for study. The case method, as pointed out above, is time-consuming. If there is a point of time in case study when diminishing educational returns set in for the student, that fact should be recognized and adjustments should be made in teaching materials and method of instruction. If it be true that such courses as economics and psychology can be studied with greater profit after the student has had the elementary law courses, then the prelaw and law programs should be rearranged to give recognition to this factor. It should be noted that the problem is one of fusion of relevant legal and non-legal subjects, and it should be noted also that the aim in shaping the program of instruction should not be that of stocking the students' minds with factual materials, but of orienting them to their surroundings, of freeing their minds, and of inculcating in them a versatility of mind for the tasks of the profession.

H. NEGLECT OF TRAINING IN PRACTICAL SKILLS

The most vocal criticism of legal education is that it is not practical enough, or stated more broadly, that it does not adequately train the young lawyer in the skills of the practice. The background of this criticism is in part historical. Apprenticeship training was the substance of English legal education; for many years it was the predominant system in America; it is the prevailing method in the Dominion of Canada,[33] in Australia,[34] and in New Zealand.[35] "If the question whether English law can be taught at the

[33] Wright, *Should the Profession Control Legal Education?* 3 J. Legal Ed. 1 (1950).

[34] *The Legal Profession and Legal Education,* 25 Aust. L. J. 441 (1951).

[35] Braybrooke, *A New Zealander Looks at American Legal Education,* 1 J. Legal Ed. 563 (1949).

Universities could be submitted in the form of a case to a body of eminent counsel," said Dicey in 1883,[36] "there is no doubt whatever as to what would be their answer. They would reply with unanimity and without hesitation that English law must be learned and cannot be taught, and that the only places where it can be learned are the law courts and chambers."

But this criticism has more substance than can be ascribed to a mere historical remnant. Apprentice training stresses the practical skills. Its weakness lies in the fact that it offers little of education in the substance and spirit of the law. It is lacking in educational versatility, perspective and vision. Even so, we cannot ignore the fact that the practice of law is a skilled craft, and that in some of its phases it is an art. The lawyer must be more than a man learned in the law and related disciplines; he must be proficient in the skills inherent in the practice of law. The criticism that there is a gap between what the young lawyer learned in school and the skills demanded of him in the practice is a valid one. Dicey, who was liberal in his praise of the American system of legal education, has commented on this subject. Referring to the Harvard Law School staff, he said,[37]

> "They rate low—a lawyer brought up under our English system is inclined to say too low—the advantage to be gained from reading in chambers. They appear slightly inclined to forget that law must always be partially a handicraft, and that even a scientific knowledge thereof is increased by the intimate acquaintance with the actual working of law which is gained from apprenticeship; if practice needs theory in order that it may

[36] Quoted by Holdsworth, *A New Discourse on the Study of the Laws* in Some Lessons from Our Legal History, 163, 171 (1928).

[37] *The Teaching of English Law at Harvard,* 13 Harv. L. Rev. 422, 429 (1900).

be intelligent, scientific theory stands in need of practice in order that it may escape unreality."

An outspoken critic of our time is Judge Jerome Frank. "I maintain," declared he,[38]

> "that something of immense worth was lost when our leading law schools wholly abandoned the legal apprentice system. I do not for a moment suggest that we return to that old system in its old form. But is it not plain that, without giving up entirely the casebook method and without discarding the invaluable alliance with the so-called 'social sciences,' our law schools should once more bring themselves into close contact with what clients need and what courts and lawyers actually do? Should the schools not execute an about-face? Should they not now adopt Judge Reeves' 18th century apprentice-school method, modifying it in the light of the wisdom gained on the long detour?"

It must not be taken, however, that the opinions of the leaders of the bench and bar are unanimous on this subject. Judge Charles E. Clark, formerly dean of the Yale Law School, is a strong champion of the efficacy of modern legal education as it is administered in the better law schools. "I regard the repetitive attempts," said he,[39]

> "to coerce law schools into offering so-called practical training as at best curiously naive, and in general at odds with sound concepts of legal education. Such attempts might be dismissed as a comparatively harmless and not unusual professional baiting of the schools except that law deans and professors are acutely attuned to professional criticism and hence may be led to waste

[38] Courts on Trial, 231 (1949).

[39] *"Practical" Legal Training an Illusion,* 3 J. Legal Ed. 423 (1951).

their substance in doing what they cannot do effectively and what if they could would not be pedagogically worth while. . . . I shall argue that law school training is now effectively efficient, more so than other types of professional education; that there is no real basis for the criticism implicit in this pressure for practical training; that the latter is limited, partial and fragmentary at best; and that the present-day legal education in problem analysis and exposition and in thorough documentation of sources is much more important and valuable, as well as more within the practical competence of the schools."

The validity of the statement that the law schools do not fully equip their graduates with the necessary skills of the profession is unassailable. Judge Clark has, however, raised a pertinent question as to what the law schools can do effectively. The implication is that the schools should undertake only those things which they are fully competent to handle. This issue has been well defined by Professor W. Barton Leach. "It is important to recognize," said he,[40]

> "that the law schools provide only one phase of a lawyer's education—the most important phase that will ever be compressed into as small a space of time as three years, but still only a phase. A lawyer's education begins in grade school or earlier and ends when he dies or retires. We take him from an earlier phase—college—and deliver him to the next phase—apprenticeship. Our question is: What ingredients of the totality of his equipment can we best supply to him in the three years he spends with us?"

The view that the things which are Caesar's should be

[40] *Property Law Taught in Two Packages,* 1 J. Legal Ed. 28, 32 (1948).

rendered unto Caesar was also vigorously stated in an address in 1911 before the Association of American Law Schools by Dean Harlan F. Stone, later Chief Justice of the Supreme Court. "Emphasis of the proper and important functions of the law school," he stressed,[41]

> "necessarily by contrast emphasizes those functions of legal training of lesser importance, or which possibly do not belong to the law school at all. Recognizing that the law school has supplanted the law office as an instrumentality for legal instruction because of its superiority in certain directions, we must also recognize that in certain other directions the law office and the court room are superior agencies for legal training. If, therefore, we attempt to do what the office can do better than the law school at the expense of the training which the law school can do better than the office, there is always danger of economic loss, not to say of wasted opportunities."

If we assume that all the graduates of law schools, on passing their bar examinations, immediately go into law offices, this argument is irrefutable. But not all law-school graduates do that. Many, indeed, do go into law offices and there serve periods of apprenticeship. But some go into the practice of law by themselves immediately upon being admitted to the bar. And this is made possible through the procedure prevailing in the various states, under which, after the neophyte has passed his bar examination and has been approved by a character and fitness committee, he is forthwith sworn in as a lawyer and given an unconditional license to practice law. We shall return to this question later.

[41] *The Function of the American University Law School*, Handbook, Ass'n Am. L. Schools, 59, 67–68 (1911). This address is also published, 36 Rep. Am. Bar Ass'n, 768, 776–777 (1911).

While the criticism that legal education is not practical enough and that it does not prepare students for the problems of the practice is a frequent one, it often is lacking in concreteness as to what the deficiencies in legal education are and as to what should be done by way of improving it. Judge Frank has charged that "most law schools omit the contacts, the face-to-face relations, with flesh-and-blood human beings, including witnesses, clients, jurors, trial judges, administrators, members of legislative committees."[42] He would have the law school build its teaching around a legal clinic. "The clinic," as he viewed it,[43]

> "would be in charge of full-time professors who had had a varied experience in practicing law. . . . The clinic's activities would thus include almost every kind of legal service rendered by law offices. Indeed, the clinic would be a law office. The students, as apprentices of the practicing-lawyer teachers, would engage in all its activities. The teacher-clinicians would discuss in detail with the student apprentices the more generalized aspects of the legal rules pertinent to the specific matters handled by the clinic."

The Survey Board that made the California study recommended an internship system, not a clinic for law students such as Judge Frank projected, but an internship superimposed on law-school training. "A law school graduate," said the Board,[44]

---

[42] *Both Ends Against the Middle*, 100 U. Pa. L. Rev. 20, 26 (1951).

[43] *Ibid.*, 29–30.

[44] Legal Education and Admissions to the Bar in California, 135–136 (1949).

"When our medical student is graduated, he is much better qualified to practice than the law school graduate. But our doctor does not hang up his shingle when he graduates. He spends from one to nine years in a hospital as an intern, working up to be a resident. If he hopes to secure a board certificate as a specialist, he has to spend at least five years as an intern and resident." Cantrall, *Economic* "who passes his bar examination is not a lawyer. . . . It is relatively easy for a high-ranking man from a 'good' law school to get a job in a big law office, where he may receive some apprentice training; yet he is the man who needs it the least. The man who completes his law work with a mediocre record in a part-time school is the forgotten man of the junior bar. It is these unapprenticed and unapprenticeable law school graduates who need first consideration. . . . If, however, the organized bar were to set up legal service offices for persons of low and medium incomes who now feel that they cannot afford legal advice, something very like legal hospitals would have been created. . . . It might then be possible to provide the kind of practical training by internship which is the greatest need of legal education today."

What is perhaps the greatest weakness of a young law-school graduate is that he is inept in dealing with facts. In the inculcation of this skill, case instruction as employed in the law schools falters. The appellate decisions the student reads have fact situations, to be sure, but they do not involve facts "in the raw" such as the lawyer must struggle with. "The facts as reported in the published decision have often gone through a triple process of distillation: unorganized 'real' facts are reduced to the facts proved in court; the facts proved in court may be reduced still further to the facts appearing in the written record on appeal; finally the facts of the written record are reduced to the facts reported by judge or reporter in the published decision."[45] The study of appellate decisions thus fails to bring home to the student

Inventory of the Legal Profession: Lawyers Can Take Lesson from Doctors, 38 A. B. A. Jour. 196, 199 (1952).

[45] Preliminary Statement of the Committee on Legal Education of the Harvard Law School, 24 (1947).

an insight into the "blood, toil, tears and sweat" involved in the lawyer's labor over facts. Case reading does not adequately discipline the neophyte for this ordeal. As a consequence the common criticism of the young lawyer is that he has not been well taught to deal with facts.

This statement finds support in a study, to which previous references have been made, by a Committee of the Harvard Law School. The Committee sent a questionnaire to a random sampling of Harvard Law School graduates. In one of the questions of this questionnaire, the Committee listed six skills, namely: "negotiation, draftsmanship, advocacy, legal planning, 'knowing the law' in a practical sense (the ability to predict how cases will be decided), and ability to secure an understanding of facts and motives. Those answering the questionnaire were asked to rank these skills in the order of their importance for the type of work they were performing."[46] The answers received yielded this significant result:[47]

> "The number of lawyers giving first rank to skill in dealing with facts was more than twice as great as that of those giving first position to any of the other skills. Averaging the numerical indices of the positions assigned these skills (so that the smaller the number reported, the higher the ranking) the relative ranking of the six skills was as follows: dealing with facts, 2.3; predicting how controversies will be decided, 3.4; legal planning, 3.4; negotiation, 3.5; draftsmanship, 3.8; advocacy, 4.1. The margin between 'dealing with facts' and the next skill in order is 1.1, while the margin between the top and the bottom in the other five skills is only 0.7. A 'sense of fact' is therefore given the highest position by a wide margin over any of the other skills."

[46] *Ibid.*, 26.
[47] *Ibid.*

We have been dealing with a broad problem that touches both legal education and admission to the bar. We start from the premise that law-school graduates, although they have passed their bar examinations, are not (or should we say, as legal education is now dispensed by the law schools, are not) *ipso facto* qualified to assume the responsibilities of the practice of law. Additional training, at least in the simpler skills of the profession, is essential. If all individuals newly admitted to the bar were required to serve office apprenticeships, or if, in fact, all took positions in offices upon their graduation from law school, the problem would tend to disappear. In a limited number of jurisdictions the standards of admission do, indeed, provide that candidates for the bar must, in addition to studying in a law school, serve office apprenticeships. In most states there is no such requirement. Whose responsibility then is it to see to it that all applicants are qualified in the essential skills of the practice? In considering this question careful thought should be given to the views expressed (as gathered from their statements above quoted) by Judge Stone, Judge Clark, and Professor Leach, that law schools should not undertake what they are not qualified or equipped to do, and particularly that they should not undertake, at the expense of training which they are qualified to give, to do something other agencies can do better than they. That position we believe is unassailable, and should become a point of departure for any further discussion on this subject. Notwithstanding, the schools have the responsibility to explore this area to determine what they, with credit to themselves, can do toward the solution of this problem. What can they do toward the better inculcation in students of a "sense of fact," toward training in legal planning and negotiation? A substantial number of law schools have already introduced courses in legal draftsmanship, but this development is still sporadic. The legal aid clinics established in some schools merit consideration.

The question before us is one of joint responsibility for the profession, the bar examiners, and the schools. These approaches to the subject suggest themselves: (1) that the schools explore what they, in accordance with sound educational policy, can do toward bridging this gap; (2) that the bar examiners introduce examinations, in addition to those they now give, to test applicants for admission on their proficiency in the simpler skills of the profession; and, as to the applicants who are unable to pass these tests, that (3) admission standards be established which would require those applicants to serve apprenticeships or internships before they can be granted licenses to practice law. A substantial number of each class newly graduating will undoubtedly be able to find positions in law offices and thus serve their apprenticeships. For those who cannot find such positions, a program of internships in connection with legal aid and perhaps in connection with lawyers' reference installations, as suggested by the California Survey, offers distinct possibilities.

I. FAILURE TO INCULCATE PROFESSIONAL STANDARDS AND IDEALS

The statement is frequently made that legal education as administered in the law schools is deficient in the teaching of ethics. The charge is founded on too narrow a premise. Learning about professional ethics does not insure ethical conduct. Ethical conduct is an expression of character—it is an expression of the inner man. The problem of ethics is not concerned with facts, but with values and objectives. Why some men are ethical in their conduct and others not involves a question of motives—of what induces some to follow one course of action and others a different one. Ethical conduct, whether it be in professional work or in dealings with one's neighbors, is a way of life.

The criticism has been made that the schools have done too little by way of introducing formal courses in legal ethics. But what do the critics mean when they insist that the schools must teach these courses? That question has caused no little confusion in the schools. "Legal ethics," as Dean Gavit has pointed out,[48] "usually connotates the subject matter contained in the Canons of Professional Ethics, and may it be said in behalf of the Law Schools that experience has demonstrated that that subject matter is not worth much of the students' and the instructors' time." It has become increasingly apparent, however, Dean Gavit went on to say,[49]

> "that the leaders of the movement for the teaching of Legal Ethics have something else in mind. Unfortunately they have employed misleading language. What they really want is not that the law schools devote more time to the teaching of the rules of Professional Ethics, but that they make some intelligent and whole-hearted attempt to develop Professional Character."

Recently Professor Elliott E. Cheatham made a careful study on this subject for the Survey of the Legal Profession.[50] He found that the attention given it by the schools is wavering and uncertain, and that the confusion mentioned by Dean Gavit still persists. In gathering the materials for his report, Professor Cheatham sent a questionnaire to all the law schools. In one of the questions inquiry was made as to whether the school addressed was offering a course on the professional functions of the lawyer. Ap-

[48] *Legal Ethics and the Law Schools*, 18 A. B. A. Jour. 326 (1932).

[49] *Ibid.*

[50] *The Inculcation of Professional Standards and the Functions of the Lawyer*, 21 Tenn. L. Rev. 812 (1951).

proximately two-thirds of the schools answered that they were giving such a course. The remainder said they were not. He felt, however, that these figures were hardly dependable, for, from the answers given, some deemed it a "course" if the school sponsored a few lectures on the formal rules of professional conduct, while others, even if such lectures were given, did not consider that those lectures could be called a "course." In the schools that gave work in this field, some devoted only three or four non-credit lectures to it; a majority gave one semester hour to it; some, two semester hours; and two, three semester hours. Where the work was offered, an average of more than fifty per cent of the students elected to take it. He found that the schools were "in almost complete verbal agreement that they should direct their efforts to professional responsibility in private practice and also to a broader sense of obligation."[51] In summarizing his findings he said:[52]

> "The majority of the replies show dissatisfaction with what the schools are doing. . . . Yet there is no semblance of uniformity in what the schools are now doing or in what they believe should be done. The variety of opinions and methods in this field is probably greater than in any other part of law school work. The variety, it appears, stems from different sources: (a) In part the disagreement is over what the function of a law school should be and over how broad should be the training it seeks to give. (b) In part, there is a difference of opinion as to the practicable methods, and scope of treatment. (c) In part, the difference is caused by the size of the schools, a seminar course being useful in small schools, and impracticable in large ones. Where the student body is small, much emphasis may be placed

[51] *Ibid.*, 816.

[52] *Ibid.*, 816–817.

> on student organizations. (d) In part, the disagreement seems to come from the attitude of the students toward the bar and the bench. Where it is respected, there may be emphasis on contact with and lectures by the bar and bench. In a more cynical or skeptical environment, this is not urged."

The situation Professor Cheatham has described is not an encouraging one. If inculcation of professional standards in students means merely introducing them to the canons of professional ethics and to a few appellate court decisions involving disciplinary proceedings against lawyers, then the answer must be an emphatic "no" to such procedure. But surely that is not the only approach to this subject. Ethical standards for the individual are born of personal conviction. The legal profession is a great creative and guiding force in society. Is it measuring up to its potentialities? What the profession is, depends upon what lawyers as individuals do. "If the law school should undertake to devote a part of its instructional program to a consideration of the future role of the legal profession," said the Harvard Committee,[53] "attention should probably be specifically directed to the following matters: (1) the basic social factors influencing the kinds of tasks the lawyer is called upon to undertake; (2) the factors influencing the growth of other professions and the balance between professions; (3) the opportunities and demands of particular branches of legal practice . . . ; (4) the lawyer's responsibility with respect to basic issues of policy, like that of economic planning."

If the question before us relates to instruction of that sort, the answer this time is an emphatic "yes." The law schools cannot escape that responsibility by debating "how broad

---

[53] Preliminary Statement of the Committee on Legal Education of the Harvard Law School, 133–134 (1947).

should be the training" they should seek to give. The role of the law schools in this area was defined with force and clarity by Justice Harlan F. Stone in an address delivered in 1934.[54] He was then Associate Justice of the Supreme Court. Previously he had been dean of one of the great law schools. He was speaking of the impact of economic and political changes on the profession—on professional standards and on the outlook and actions of individual lawyers. The picture he portrayed was one of changing, if not faltering, professional standards. He then turned his attention to university law schools and to what they might do to promote the highest interests of the bar. "There is opportunity, too," said he,[55]

> "for a new emphasis in the training of the young men who, thronging the lecture rooms of the law schools today, will give character and direction to our profession tomorrow. From the beginning the law schools have steadily raised their intellectual standards. It is not too much to say that they have worshipped the proficiency which they have sought and attained to a remarkable degree. But there is grave danger to the public if this proficiency be directed wholly to private ends without thought of social consequences, and we may well pause to consider whether the professional school has done well to neglect so completely the inculcation of some knowledge of the social responsibility which rests upon a public profession. I do not refer to the teaching of professional ethics. I have no thought that men are made moral by the mere formulation of rules of conduct, no matter how solemnly bar associations may pronounce them, or that they may be made good by

[54] Dedicatory Exercises of the Law Quadrangle, University of Michigan, 47 (1934); this address also published, *The Public Influence of the Bar*, 48 Harv. L. Rev. 1 (1934).

[55] *Ibid.*, Dedicatory Exercises, 63–64; Harv. L. Rev. 13–14.

mere exhortation. But men serve causes because of their devotion to them. The zeal of the student for proficiency in the law, like that of his elder brother at the Bar, comes from a higher source than selfishness. It is devotion to his conception of a useful and worthy institution. But that conception is a distorted one if it envisages only the cultivation of skill without thought of how and to what end it is to be used, and the question what the law schools have done and can do to make that conception truer is one to be pondered and to be answered. It is not beyond the power of institutions which have so successfully mastered the art of penetrating all the intricacies of legal doctrine to impart a truer understanding of the functions of those who are to be its servants. That understanding will come, not from platitudinous exhortation, but from knowledge of the consequences of the failure of a profession to bear its social responsibilities, and what it is doing and may do to meet them."

We shall return to a discussion of this subject in the next chapter.

VIII. LEGAL EDUCATION—A PRESENT APPRAISEMENT

One of the first decisions the Council of the Survey of the Legal Profession made, during its initial deliberations on its assignment, was that there should be a personal inspection of all the law schools in the United States. This undertaking was placed under the immediate supervision of Mr. John G. Hervey, Adviser to the Council of the Section of Legal Education and Admissions to the Bar of the American Bar Association. The inspections were made by Mr. Hervey and a group of individuals selected to assist him.[1] Mr. Hervey has the assignment of correlating the results of these inspections. I shall not encroach on his undertaking other than to assimilate into this study the reflective thinking on legal education of the men who made the inspections.

A. Objectives and Pertinent Appraisals of Legal Education

In the record of their impressions we note, first of all, the conclusion of the inspectors that law-school faculties have done all too little thinking in terms of aims and objectives in legal education. In 1947 the Committee on Curriculum of the Association of American Law Schools projected a symposium at the annual meeting of the Association on "Purpose, Program and Method in Legal Education."[2] Under the head-

[1] The individuals who participated in the inspections with Mr. Hervey were: Elliott E. Cheatham, Laurence W. DeMuth, Shelden D. Elliott, John C. Fitzgerald, Lon L. Fuller, Milton D. Green, Orlando J. Hollis, Frank E. Horack, Jr., Gordon W. Johnston, Robert A. Leflar, John W. Morland, Charles B. Nutting, Lawrence Park, John Ritchie, III, Will Shafroth, George Neff Stevens, Russell N. Sullivan, and Henry B. Witham.

[2] Outline distributed at the session (1947).

ing, "What are the aims and objectives of legal education?", the Committee proposed six questions for discussion, namely: "(1) To orient the student in relation to the problems, materials and methods of the law? (2) To fortify the student with as much basic information as may be essential to a working knowledge of the law? (3) To practice the student in the more important craft skills of the law? (4) To instruct the student in the nature and scope of the law as a system? (5) To inculcate an understanding of social background and of the law's relation to its purpose? (6) To cultivate sensitivity to professional responsibilities and an appreciation of the lawyer's place in society?" This was a most encouraging approach to what must be looked upon as a core question in legal education. Unfortunately after the symposium there was no follow-up on this subject on the part of the Association.

In fairness to the schools we should state that the feeling among law teachers is that they are constantly dealing with questions relating to aims and objectives. What they have done is to approach this subject interstitially, piecemeal and not comprehensively. Some schools have, indeed, subjected their programs of instruction to searching analysis, for example, a study made by the law faculty of Columbia University in the late 1920's, and one made by the Committee on Legal Education of the Harvard Law School in 1947, but these have been rare undertakings. The inspections disclose that soul-searching of this sort is almost nonexistent among the schools; that but a minor fraction of them even have committees on curriculum; and that only a pitiful few have committees on aims and objectives. This situation in the schools, we must conclude, shows a major weakness in legal education.

"Judging from my experience, both in connection with the Survey and otherwise," commented one inspector,

> "law schools fall roughly into three broad categories. One, those which are doing an inadequate job and which do not give value received to the students in exchange for their tuition; two, schools which perform the routine work of basic legal instruction well enough but which are completely orthodox and conventional in their outlook; and three, schools which not only perform their tasks of basic instruction, but which also are constantly alert for new opportunities and are continually attempting to extend the field of their influence."

It was his judgment that the schools in the second category are by far the most numerous. He then went on to make this appraisal:

> "Law schools are becoming increasingly aware of the fact that their obligation to the community extends far beyond the training of students for the practice of law. To a considerable extent, law schools are participating in programs of continuing legal education. In addition, some schools . . . are developing programs of organized research pointing toward the solution of difficult social problems."

A more severe, but not necessarily inconsistent, observation was recorded by another inspector: "Of the nine schools I inspected, six showed no impact of the modern world, whatsoever."

(1) QUANTITY AND QUALITY

The inspector last quoted noted the advances in legal education in the last twenty-five years, most of them mechanical and pedestrian. Among those he listed were: the substantial elimination of the commercial school; the increase of quantitative prelegal requirements from two to three years; some increase in graduation requirements; scme quantitative improvements in the facilities of the schools. As against this background he pointed to areas which should have attention but are not getting it. "The attempt to evaluate law schools on a quantitative basis," he contended,

> "should be relegated to secondary importance. The temptation to use mechanical standards is great . . . but there is only slight evidence that the mechanical . . . improvement in our law schools has resulted in any substantial improvement in legal education measured by the requirements of the society which legal education serves. Attention should be given to the curriculum. To date, curricular change has involved a little pruning, much addition . . . and a little reorganization reflecting the changed needs of the legal profession. . . . I personally feel it is more important to modernize old courses than to add new ones. . . . All these steps highlight the fact that the single most important need of legal education today is finance."

Progress in legal education, as we have seen, has been brought about through the establishment of certain quantitative standards—through setting up requirements involving specified periods of prelaw and law study, minimum physical facilities for law schools, the number of books in law-school libraries, the minimum number of teachers on law-school staffs, and so on. Several of the inspectors have pointed out that these standards are now yielding diminishing returns, and that one of the next major moves for improvement in legal education and in the standards of admission to the bar must be through emphasis on the criterion of quality. The objective in legal education is to produce well-trained and capable lawyers—lawyers who are skilled in legal procedures, who are versatile in the tasks of the law, who have an understanding and a vision of the purposes and mission of the law, and who are guided by a sense of moral responsibility. The traits we are describing involve quality, but legal education cannot produce candidates for the bar who have those traits unless the standards bearing on the admission of students to the law schools, on graduation from the law schools, and on admission to the bar, emphasize the factor of quality. One of the weaknesses in legal education and in the standards of admission to the bar is that the quality criterion has not been adequately stressed.

(2) SCHOOLS INADEQUATELY FINANCED

It is common knowledge that law schools are poorly financed, but it appears that it requires first-hand information on the unhappy results of inadequate financial support for legal education to engender a fighting conviction on that subject. One inspector expressed the view that the principal difficulties in legal education can all be traced to the fact that law schools do not have sufficient funds with which to operate. "More money," said he, "could cure many ills of which we are perfectly aware, but which we are impotent ourselves to correct." Another commented:

> "In order to participate in new developments in legal education, generous financial support is necessary. This is true largely because programs involving seminars, legal writing and organized research can be conducted only with small groups of students and therefore the proportion of faculty members to students must be considerably higher than that which is usually found in American law schools. An additional factor is the expense of developing adequate library facilities for programs of this nature. Traditionally, law schools have been very largely self-supporting and it is difficult to convince university administrations that legal education must be heavily subsidized."

The cost of medical education is often contrasted with that of legal education. "The Flexner Report," observed an inspector, "made clear to the medical profession that they could not achieve first-rate medical instruction without expanding the financial support of medical schools many, many fold. . . . If law schools are to assert the same type of influence for the improvement of the legal order, law-school finance must achieve some type of parity with medical-school finance. It is pathetic to read law-school budgets and at the same time listen to law-school administrators discuss legal research and realize that no research of consequence can ever be achieved within the framework of the financial support the school is receiving. Indeed, the present financial support of a great majority of law schools is inadequate to maintain a minimum instructional program."

The lack of adequate financial support, we conclude, is a conspicuous weakness in legal education. The successive steps in the evolution of legal education—from apprentice training to practitioner-conducted classes, to law schools cheaply administered, to university programs of legal education and research—project this problem into relief, both as to why legal education has been cheap and why, if it is to meet the needs of society for law and order, appropriations for its support must be increased manyfold. The need for this development is imperative; vastly greater sums of money must be devoted to the education of future lawyers and to legal research.

(3) PROBLEM OF LARGE CLASSES

Several of the men who made the inspections laid stress on the fact that law-school classes often are too large. This, in part, can be ascribed to the constant pressure to make legal education cheap. Said one inspector, "Classes are too large," and there is "no sound program for counselling students." "Generally speaking," observed another, "law-school classes are too large. . . . Written exercises and tests from which the student would derive profit are not required in large classes because of the tremendous burden of paper work they impose on the instructor." "Basically," commented still another, "the difficulty with legal education as compared with modern medical education is that the law schools have been mass producers operating on a low cost basis. It is characteristic of the law schools that their students are taught in large classes without much opportunity for supervised individual work." We need not elaborate further. The criticism that classes as conducted in many law schools are too large for educational efficiency is a valid one.

(4) COMMENTS ON PRELEGAL EDUCATION

The status of prelegal education and the problem of the fusion of non-legal and legal materials remain among the foremost questions confronting modern legal education. We have previously dealt at some length with this subject. The views we sought to express have support in the findings of the inspectors. The comments of two of them are illustrative. "No satisfactory solution," said one, "has been found to prelegal education on the college level. Perhaps there is no solution but I fancy that many of us are embarrassed in justifying the B.A. or three-year requirement for admission, as presently administered." The other, after offering some general comments, directed his attention specifically to the subject of prelegal work. "Let me turn next," said he,

> "to weaknesses in the *total* training of law students. I have found that some schools still approach legal education as if it were confined to that small segment of the total training which is in direct charge of law teachers in the three-year period of the students' attendance in the college of law. Most law schools, as their catalogues give evidence, shrug off any real concern with the prelegal training of their students, and in no way attempt to take care of weaknesses in that segment of

the total training. We law-school men talk glibly about the necessity for the integration of the humanities, the social sciences, and the natural sciences with law, but we haven't yet done the hard thinking and taken the difficult steps that will actually give some assurances that that necessary integration in fact takes place in the training of our students."

(5) OVERCROWDED CURRICULUM

The law-school curriculum is overcrowded with course offerings. That has long been a factor of concern to the law schools. The orthodox period of law study is, and has been for some time, three years. The lawyer who studied law near the beginning of the present century will recall that the curriculum even then seemed crowded. Nearly all the courses then taught still have a place, in one form or another, in the present curriculum, but since then there have been injected into the program several new and major courses touching the developing fields of the law, for example, taxation, administrative law, trade regulation, and labor law. The law schools have fretted over this question but they have not come to grips with it. From the point of view of the student who seeks a comprehensive program of instruction, little or nothing is solved through the addition of new courses to the curriculum. If he takes this course he must leave out that one, and so on. Some progress has been made through the consolidation and telescoping of courses, and through the setting up of so-called "core courses" covering the work of the first two years, and leaving the third year open to students for a free election of courses. Law teachers agree that the case method of instruction is time-consuming. If it be true, as we have previously implied, that the case method has had its maximum educational impact by the end of the student's first year of law study, then the way is open for different and perhaps more rapid methods of instruction during his second and third years. The law schools have given some but only sporadic attention to moves of this sort.

The problems of the curriculum are complicated yet further, and substantially so, through injections into it (in addition to instruction in fields representative of the emergent law mentioned above) of two highly divergent types of courses. One of these is responsive to the pressure, of respected lineage, that legal education must have breadth and wide perspective. This pressure has resulted in the introduction into the curriculum of such courses as law and the economic order, the criminal law and the public order, international law, law and society, welfare legislation, comparative law, legal history, jurisprudence, the philosophy of the law, and the history of the legal profession and its role in society. The other is responsive to the demands that the teaching of law must be made more practical. This pressure has stimulated the setting up of so-called "skill courses," for example, legal writing, legal drafting, legislation and the legislative process, legal accounting, fact finding, and the establishment of legal aid clinics.

All this the schools, or many of them, are attempting to pour into the ancient measure—the three-year course of study. What is resulting is something just this side of chaos. The import of this situation did not escape the inspectors. The trouble is, remarked one, "that most teachers have lost their faith in the old dialectic case analysis *as a legal philosophy,* that is, as an explanation of how law does and should work; they have not been able to develop new teaching methods that will present the same stimulus to students, and keep the same focus in the discussion, and at the same time avoid the philosophic limitations of the older . . . . conception." As viewed by another inspector, the "difficulty is that the teachers of law as a class have been unwilling to rework their courses to include the modern material. The explanation is," said he, "that there isn't enough time to teach the old law, and, I might add, there never was and never will be." Commented yet another,

> "During the past quarter of a century there has been an enormous expansion in the area of a lawyer's responsibility. Law-school curricula have expanded accordingly. But, in most schools, the length of time required for the LL.B. degree has not been increased since the turn of the century. Most schools are still three-year schools. Typically, course offerings in these schools total a great many more hours than a student can take in three academic years. This means that students do not receive formal instruction in important and ofttimes basic subjects. . . . I look for an increasing number of schools to increase their present programs from three academic years to three academic years and one or two summer sessions."

Three approaches toward the solution of the problem suggest themselves: (1) a reorganization of the law curriculum involving drastic measures of consolidation and elimination; (2) a fusion of prelegal and legal work involving a more efficient employment of the prelegal years. This would require much reorganization, but it merits serious consideration from the point of view both of conserving time and of fostering sound educational policy; and (3) the extension of the period of law study beyond the orthodox three years. All three approaches, probably, should be explored at the same time. Of the three, the extension of the period of law study is, perhaps, the least desirable, but it is the approach to the problem that is most likely to be taken. Nine schools (exclusive of several that have introduced four-year programs based on two years of prelegal work) have already lengthened their programs, some to three years and a semester, some to three and one-third years, and some to three years and an eight-week summer session.

(6) PUBLIC LAW

Closely related to the issues raised in the foregoing discussion, and posing a basic question of educational policy, is the demand that the schools give greater emphasis to the teaching of public law. "It has been asserted," noted the Harvard Committee,[3] "that the great emphasis given private law in our curriculum and that of other law schools is out of keeping with the demands of modern law practice, and that in this respect legal education presents the spectacle of a serious cultural lag." The replies to the questionnaire sent out in relation to its study confirmed, said the Committee,[4] "the general judgment that this branch of law has a greater importance in practice than it does in legal education." A comment on this subject by one of the inspectors admirably sums up the situation. "Increasingly," said he,

> "the study of law is an accepted mode of preparation for public service, particularly in the field of governmental administration. In addition, the nature of the lawyer's function in society makes him in many respects a public servant *ex officio*. In a substantial number of law schools there has been a fair appreciation of these facts, and a reorganization of the curriculum accordingly. But this has not been true of all law schools. In many schools a considerable number of relatively unimportant but traditional private law courses are continued in the curriculum, more because of inertia than any other reason, while new public law courses, courses in which public and private law coalesce, or courses emphasiz-

[3] Preliminary Statement of the Committee on Legal Education of the Harvard Law School, 80 (1947). A discerning study on this subject is Brown, Lawyers, Law Schools and the Public Service (1948); a helpful shorter study, made for the Survey of the Legal Profession, is Ford, The Government Lawyer (1952).

[4] Harvard Study, *ibid.*

ing the public nature of the legal profession are still neglected."

B. BRIDGING THE GAP BETWEEN LAW SCHOOLS AND PRACTICE

One of the most troublesome questions that confront legal education relates to the problem of bridging the gap between the law schools and the practice. That problem persists today. I have previously devoted some attention to it and there ventured the opinion that it is one of joint responsibility for the profession, the bar examiners and the law schools. I expressed the view that the obligation rests on the schools to give their attention to this subject, and beyond what the schools might do toward its solution, that applicants for admission to the bar might be required, after finishing their law-school studies, to serve for a period as apprentices in law offices or as interns in connection with legal aid programs before they are given an unqualified license to practice law. For the moment we are concerned with an appraisal of this problem as it touches the schools. Later I shall wish to describe some steps the schools are now taking toward its solution.

In discussing this issue we are confronted first of all with the question as to what is involved in bridging the gap between the schools and the practice. All who are concerned with this question, the critics and the schools, agree that there is a gap. But what is it that the young graduate lacks in his training to equip him for the practice? On this question there is no clear agreement. Some seem to stress the fact that he is wanting in skills of legal procedure—in the ability to handle even simple trial work. That probably is true, but others contend that this weakness is relatively unimportant; that what the neophyte really is wanting in is skill in dealing with facts—that he has no conception as to how to get and how to handle "raw facts"; and that he is lacking in the skills of draftsmanship and negotiation.

(1) THE LEGAL CLINIC

Among the measures that have been initiated to assist the young man in bridging the gap between school and practice, and as to the merits of which there is some difference of opinion, is that of the legal clinic. One of the advisers on this study has well stated the case for the clinic as an educational device. "It is feasible," said he,

> "to set up legal aid as a part of a law-school program so that it has educational substance. There is a *science* of law; that you now teach. There is an *art* of practice; that you now do not teach. That art can be learned only by *doing*. The doing must be with live cases, viz. with human beings. . . . Although the student's time in law school is limited, there is time for clinical training. . . . Clinical training is an essential part of learning to deal with problems. The men are not going to find their problems in books and they are not going to devote their lives to arguing cases on appeal. The facts are not going to come to them in neatly printed records. . . . Legal aid, if extended as it must be, can provide clinical material for a great many students. . . . We do have statistics as to what most students do on graduation. They go out for themselves. Right now more than 66% of our lawyers are practicing solo. . . . If training in practice is not the duty of the law schools," he asked pointedly, "whose duty is it?" He then added, "It may be that clinical training will have to come after law school and *before* admission."

Quintin Johnstone, who made a study on this subject for the Survey, found that "there is little consensus in any of the groups [law-school teachers, legal aid societies, and bar associations] concerned with legal education or legal aid as to the desirability of legal aid clinics."[5] "It seems to me," commented an adviser on this study, "that many legal aid clinics are based on the assumption that the practice of law is much as it was thirty or forty years ago; that is, adversary proceeding existing in a small community when the courthouse was the center of the law. Many men will have but limited use for much of the training in the legal aid clinic." Professor John S. Bradway, the tireless pioneer in this field, has summarized the principal arguments for and against this institution. Said he,[6]

> "It seems that no one has gone so far as to meet the legal aid clinic proposal head on and declare flatly that 'a program for student work' in connection with flesh and blood clients and real cases is without merit. Rather the comments are oblique. They fall naturally into three groups, in effect: (a) we do not see the value of the program; (b) we have enough trouble already with a crowded law school curriculum without adding to it; (c) the 'material' (clients and cases) used for educational purposes which is made available to the student through legal aid clinics has only limited value because it is not sufficiently representative of general law practice. Preliminarily by way of reply, one may suggest that these objections are not insuperable. The value of the program readily may be made clearer; eventually

[5] *Law School Legal Aid Clinics*, 3 J. Legal Ed. 533, 539 (1951). This subject is also touched upon in a wider study on legal aid, made for the Survey, Brownell, Legal Aid in the United States, 107–109 (1951). The view that a law-school education should be supplemented by apprentice training before an applicant for the profession is given a license to practice is vigorously supported in another study for the Survey of the Legal Profession. Reginald Heber Smith, Legal Service Offices for Persons of Moderate Means, pamph., 36–47 (1951).

[6] *The Second Mile for Legal Aid Clinics*, 1952 Wash. U. L. Q. 165, 166–167.

the problem of the crowded curriculum, irrespective of the impact upon it of the legal aid clinic movement, will have to be faced and not evaded, why not now; and an alert imaginative legal aid clinic staff, without undue exertion, may supply the students with 'material' which a reasonable man would regard as representative of general law practice."

A highly persuasive argument for the clinics is stated by Quintin Johnstone. "The group that seems to be most solidly in favor of legal aid clinics," said he,[7]

> "is made up of lawyers in practice who did clinic work as law students. Questionnaires recently were sent to representative groups of former legal aid students at the University of Minnesota Law School and the University of Cincinnati Law School. Responses were requested to a series of questions relating to the value of clinic work to those questioned and recommended improvements in the clinic programs. The responses received were unanimous to the effect that the clinic experience was of value to those questioned, and the most frequent recommendation for change was that the students spend more time in such work."

(2) THE RESPONSIBILITY OF THE SCHOOLS

We have emphasized the fact that the law schools must assume the responsibility, as the accepted overseers of legal education, of giving their attention to the training of students in the practical as well as the analytical skills of the lawyer. "Bear in mind," bluntly said an adviser on this study, "that the law schools have insisted on a monopoly of legal education. . . . The dilemma is one that the law schools have created for themselves. If they will say, after honest consideration, that they are unfit for such teaching

[7] *Law School Legal Aid Clinics*, supra, note 5, p. 540.

then it will be up to the courts and the profession to take charge and devise some alternative plan." We must not take it from this that the schools have not already moved into this field. Some, indeed, have done very little on this subject, but others have been keenly aware of the problem, and have worked to bring about a solution. Notwithstanding, this remains a blind spot in legal education. The legal aid clinic clearly merits consideration. It should be evaluated as an educational measure, and appraised by the criterion stated years ago by Harlan F. Stone. The law schools should not attempt to do what some other agency can do better than they, at the expense of training which the schools can do better than any other agency. From what has already been done successfully by the schools, it seems clear that they can go yet further in the inculcation of practical skills. It is not unlikely that they will be able to go all the way in bridging the gap between law study and the practice, but failing that, then they should frankly acknowledge that some other agency or agencies must step in to finish the task. In that event, clinical training through office apprenticeships or internships in connection with legal aid programs might be required after graduation from law school and before admission to the bar.

C. PART-TIME SCHOOLS

Part-time legal education, once the subject of heated controversy, still draws some but substantially less fire than it formerly did. We are dealing here with the problem of the night and late afternoon schools. Only relatively few schools hold late afternoon classes exclusively. Of the total of 124 law schools approved by the American Bar Association, 40 conduct night programs. Of these, 34 run both full-time day and part-time night work; six hold only night classes. Thirty-nine law schools are unapproved by the American Bar Association. Of these, three hold only morning classes;

four hold both day and night classes; and 32 have only night classes.

The principal criticisms, in the past, of part-time schools were that they conducted inadequate educational programs; that their standards of scholarship were low; and that they were poorly financed and were operated for commercial purposes.[8] Some of these criticisms are still relevant, at least as to some of the part-time schools, and they are particularly pertinent as to many of the unapproved schools. The part-time schools were given the indicia of respectability in 1921 through the adoption by the American Bar Association of the now-famous recommendations sponsored by a special committee of which Elihu Root was chairman,[9] and through the resolutions adopted the following year by the Conference of Bar Association Delegates.[10] The actions taken at those meetings specified that the course of law study should be three years for students who give substantially all their working time to their law studies "and a longer course, equivalent in the number of working hours, if they devote only part of their working time to their studies."[11]

The separate statements of two of the inspectors of the law schools for the Survey cogently present the current arguments against and for part-time legal education. "Another limiting factor," said one,

> "raises what to my mind is one of the most serious problems facing us. This is the matter of part-time legal education, particularly as conducted in night schools. I am strongly of the opinion that programs of the sort mentioned in the preceding paragraph [seminars, legal writing, and organized research] cannot be conducted effectively except in a full-time institution. Thus, al-

---

[8] Brown, Lawyers and the Promotion of Justice, 38–45 (1938).

[9] 46 Rep. Am. Bar Ass'n, 661–678, 679, 687–688 (1921).

[10] 47 Rep. Am. Bar Ass'n, 482–484 (1922).

[11] 46 Rep. Am. Bar Ass'n, 687 (1921).

though adequate conventional legal education may be conducted in a night school, there is, in my opinion, a very serious question as to whether any night school, no matter how sincerely it may endeavor to do so, can really do an effective job under modern conditions. In spite of the hardship which such a course would work on many worthy and sincere persons, it seems to me the time has come to give serious consideration to the complete abolition of part-time legal education, at least in preparation for the practice of law."

The other inspector commented,

"The part-time law school's place in legal education should be stressed. More and more because of economic conditions students are finding it necessary to work while in school. Part-time legal education can be every bit as good as full-time legal education. Several law schools are demonstrating this very clearly. Two essentials must be met. First, the teachers must be of the same caliber and as fully devoted to teaching as the full-time day-school teachers. Second, the students must be held to exactly the same high standards as the full-time students. They must be required to carry and do equally well, work involving use of the library, research, drafting, moot court, legal aid, or anything else required of full-time students. A third essential may be indicated and that is that the part-time students' load must be kept within bounds."

The status of part-time legal education is prejudiced in a substantial measure by the fact that many of the inferior schools are in that category. They represent the closest approach of our day to the practitioner-conducted schools of an earlier era. It is a cheap way to run a law school. We should observe, however, that a substantial number of part-time schools are now administered under the aegis of universities and are fully approved by the American Bar Association, and that some that have no university affiliations are likewise approved by that Association. Mr. A. Z. Reed has made a good appraisal of the situation. "From a political point of view," said he, writing in 1928,[12] the part-time law schools,

> "render an undoubted service. Because of the existence of these institutions, and only because of their existence, we are certain to escape not the least of the dangers that the hideous complexity of American law has brought in its train. This is that the preparation of American lawyers should become so expensive that access to the legal profession would be virtually restricted to the well-to-do. But the same educational machinery that has been developed with this laudable objective has brought with it its own evils. Access to the legal profession is one thing; over-easy access, quite another. Evening law schools have made it possible for young men to be admitted to the bar who ought to have been admitted and who otherwise could not have been. But they have also served to inject into the profession young men who have injured both themselves and the community by embarking upon this career; in some cases because they were not the stuff out of which good lawyers can be made, in other cases because they have been led to choose the easy road rather than make the additional sacrifice required to attend a good full-time school."

Subject to allowance for the fact that part-time legal education has, in the last quarter of a century, been im-

[12] Present-Day Law Schools in the United States and Canada, 289 (Carneg. Found. Bul. 21, 1928).

proved substantially in many part-time schools, Reed's appraisal is persuasive and substantially sound.[13]

D. FERMENT IN THE LAW SCHOOLS

Throughout this study we have given our attention, in the main, to a critical appraisal of legal education. The story would not be complete without recording some encouraging developments. There is today a substantial measure of activity and ferment in the law schools. Never before in the long history of legal education has there been so much self-criticism among law teachers as there is now. This state of mind has not permeated into all the schools, but it is widespread and it is genuine. Law teachers in substantial numbers are active in the sense of being willing to engage in educational experiments. Many of these experiments, no doubt, are ephemeral, but the happy fact is that they are being undertaken. Some, indeed, are significant and have already resulted in the introduction of courses and educational programs that are occupying permanent spots in the curricula of a number of schools.

This appraisal finds support in the reflective comments of the men who inspected the schools for the Survey. They stressed a variety of developments, all of which are indicative of the ferment now in process. "I doubt," conjectured one, "that there is any other field of traditional educational endeavor in which there has been greater willingness to attempt new techniques." He then mentioned some experimental developments, and among them legal aid clinics, legal writing courses, practice courts, and visual aids. "The trend," commented another,

"is away from the case book as I knew it as a student

[13] The program of part-time schools is well described in a study for the Survey, Nicholson, *Some Problems of Metropolitan Law Schools Having Day and Night Divisions*, 4 J. Legal Ed. 141 (1951).

some 25 years ago. Many modern case books contain a substantial amount of text material. Some progress is being made toward including relevant social science materials in these books. More attention is being placed on the economic and social matrix of problems presented by the cases discussed in class. The 'problem method of approach' is gaining adherence. More emphasis is being placed on acquainting students with the full sweep of a transaction from initial interview with the client to final disposition by the appellate court. Also, more emphasis is being placed on trial, appellate, and office practice, on drafting legal instruments and on training students to write clearly, concisely and accurately. Possibly, too, more is being done in alerting students to their responsibilities as citizens and potential civic leaders, and to discussing with them the basic values in a democratic society."

Relative to the criticism that the law schools do not prepare men for the practice, one of the inspectors properly pointed out that, as commonly stated, this complaint is too sweeping; that it tends to prove too much. The schools are indeed, he contended, doing a good job in the inculcation of analytical powers. The criticism is valid, however, that the schools have neglected training as to various practical skills. As to these, his observation was that the schools have today awakened to their full responsibility. "While emphasizing analytical skills and advocacy as formerly," said he,

"the law schools are now making a real effort towards solving the problem of transition of the student from law school to practice. Skill courses which gave the student some training in the drafting of simple legal instruments, of memoranda on points of law (formerly limited to law-review men), fuller and more complete

> moot court work, including not only the traditional appellate trial, but also evidence, the drafting of pleadings, and of briefs, and even some effort at motion practice and pretrial procedures, are lending to realism in legal education. . . . Many schools are experimenting with courses in office management, legal aid clinics, seminars, briefing services, indigent prisoner assistance work, and required supervised visits to County Recorders' Offices and to actual trials. All these efforts are aimed at showing the law student not only the law in action but how vital his knowledge of theory actually is in the solution of a client's problem."

We must not overdraw this picture. We are describing only the ferment that is in process in the law schools and the trends in legal education. Even so, these are important facts for the record. What is today taking place in the law schools is adequate material for a separate and exciting story. Legislation, long neglected, is now an integral field of study, and is firmly installed in the programs of a substantial number of schools. The legal clinic is still in a tentative stage but there is widespread interest in it and it has been installed in a number of schools. Legal writing and exposition is a course that has made a place for itself in various programs. Experiments are in progress in several schools with visual aids. As might be expected, these experiments are being developed principally in the leading law schools, but they are by no means restricted to those schools. Some of the most promising projects have originated in the smaller schools.

The problem of large classes is being alleviated in several schools through two constructive educational measures: first, through tutorial programs introduced into the first year of law study, under which small groups of the first-year class are assigned to teaching fellows or associates for personal guidance and individual instruction in areas of study methods, legal writing and legal research; second, through the seminar method of instruction. This is confined to advanced students, ordinarily to students in their senior year of law study.

The seminar has become a common instrument of instruction. It is restricted to small groups of from ten to fifteen students. A colleague has given me this brief statement of the seminar conducted by him in federal taxation. To enroll in this course the student must have previously had the basic course in federal taxation. The following objectives underlie the course:

> "One is to enable the student to increase his store of information relating to principles of federal taxation. Another is to provide an opportunity for both intensive and comprehensive research in federal tax law. The third is to afford experience in legal writing. The fourth objective, which is implicit in those previously stated, is to develop skill in the use of the research tools of federal tax law. To achieve these objectives the student, during the course of the semester, is given a series of assignments or problems. These are of a functional nature and are assigned to focus attention upon tax problems inherent in transactions frequently encountered in the practice. The following are cited in general terms as illustrative of a few transactions which provide the basis for assigned problems: operation, dissolution and liquidation of partnerships; death of a partner; organization and liquidation of corporations; use of life insurance in financing the purchase of business interests at death; the improvement of real estate by a life tenant. The student is required to state a solution of the problem presented and to prepare a supporting memorandum

> of the type customary in the practice. These papers provide the basis for oral reports by the student and discussion in the seminar. In addition to the regular assignments, each student is required to prepare a lengthy research paper upon some topic of federal taxation comparable to a law-review article."

A valid criticism of legal education has been that the law student, though steeped in case law through the reading of many appellate decisions, does not learn how to get and how to deal with "raw facts." The shift in emphasis in the seminars from case analysis to problem solution holds forth promise that this weakness in legal education can be overcome. A correspondent has given me an interesting statement on his approach to the teaching of a seminar in property law. "After an introductory series of lectures," in the words of his description,

> "on the relationship between a restrictive covenant running with the land and the general provisions of zoning ordinances, the members of the seminar are given particular problems involving tracts of land or lots in the city . . . and asked to prepare necessary papers to achieve particular uses of the land or to resist them. In this process the students learn the mechanical operations of the city engineer's office, the clerk-treasurer's office, the board of public works, the city council, the county surveyor's office, the county clerk and county recorder, as well as the city and county plan commissions and board of zoning appeals. They must also, of course, be familiar with the state statutes, state administrative regulations relating particularly to specialized businesses such as dry cleaning establishments, filling stations and the like, and regulations of the state highway commission and ordinances of the city and county. My primary objective, of course, is the sub-

stantive one of teaching the young lawyer the problems of land use planning and how it affects real estate transactions. But incident to the substantive knowledge, he acquires an understanding of the forms involved and is forced to go to all of the offices and, I hope, get over the general reticence that a young lawyer has of exposing his ignorance in asking a public official to help him out."[14]

While there is a heavy emphasis today, as evidenced by the experiments in progress, on skill training and on "how" courses, what impresses the observer even more is the diversity of trends in modern legal education. There is a marked stress on the broader and more cultural areas—on a synthesis of the law and a fusion of legal and nonlegal materials. This movement finds expression in various ways. One is through changes in the content of casebooks. The modern casebook, as I have heretofore noted, bears little resemblance to the casebook of an earlier era. It no longer is a work made up exclusively of cases. Instead its content consists of cases interspersed with relevant readings and text materials from the area of the social sciences. To bring legal education into a closer relationship with the social sciences, some law schools have added economists, psychologists, and other specialists to their

[14] These are but fragments of evidence bearing on the immense amount of experimentation that is now going on in the law schools. I had hoped to give a fairly complete description in the present study of this area of activity. I have statements in my files from many individuals, to whom I am very grateful, descriptive of the ferment now in process. I found, if I were to devote the attention to this subject which it deserves, that it would throw the overall study on legal education, which I am attempting to make, out of focus. The experiments that are in progress are extremely fascinating. It is as if law teachers had suddenly been released from bondage. This area deserves careful analysis and appraisal. I express the hope that someone will undertake that task.

staffs. It is indeed true, as one of the advisers to this study remarked, "current law-school trends are many and varied." He noted,

> "a trend toward greater emphasis on synthesis than has been true in the past. Related to this is the emphasis on the knowledge of rules of law, the use of text material presented in law review articles, in the Restatements, and in textbooks. Certainly there is a strong trend toward the introduction of more so-called non-legal materials."

In this period of transition and change, the *Journal of Legal Education* deserves mention as an instrumentality that has played a significant role in the stimulation of experimentation in the law schools. The *Journal* is devoted exclusively to matters relating to legal education. It is published quarterly by the Association of American Law Schools. Though it has been published for only a comparatively short period—it made its first appearance in the autumn of 1948—it has proven to be a clearing house of information on matters of legal education. The insertion in it of a division headed "Law School Developments," where anyone who thinks he has an idea about legal education may have his say, was a master stroke. The materials appearing in the *Journal,* and particularly those printed under the "Developments" heading, are highly provocative.

What are the implications of these developments? The atmosphere of excitement found in many of the schools today augurs well for legal education. Law teachers are alert to the broad implications of legal education as they never have been before, except, perhaps, during the formative years of the Republic. But there also is an atmosphere of confusion. As if by common agreement law teachers no longer feel the restraints of the old dialectic of case analysis, but they have not found a substantive replacement for it. Present objectives for legal education are not clear. The educational experiments now in progress, while indicative of a salutary state of affairs, need evaluation as to their relative educational content. What is more, major problems, touching the conservation of the students' prelegal years, the fusion of legal and non-legal materials, and the overall length of the period of study in preparation for the bar, remain unsolved.

E. RAPPROCHEMENT BETWEEN LAW TEACHERS AND PRACTICING LAWYERS

Another development relates to the rapprochement between law teachers and the practicing members of the profession. We must revert to the apprenticeship days of legal education for anything comparable, but under the apprenticeship system the lawyer was the law teacher. After the gravitation of legal education to the universities and particularly after the advent of Langdell, who insisted that law teachers, in order to do an effective job as teachers and scholars, must devote their full time to this undertaking, a new branch of the legal profession came into being—that of the professional law teacher. This was one of the most salutary developments in the history of legal education. But incidental to it there grew up an estrangement between the teacher and the practitioner. The teaching group instead of becoming an integral branch of the profession took on attributes of a species quite distinct. Practicing lawyers and law teachers mingled only on rare occasions. If the practicing lawyer thought of the law teacher at all, he viewed him all too frequently as an impractical theorist. That this would result in a breach between the schools and the profession was inevitable. That a breach did develop and that it had unfortunate implications not only for the law teachers but for the whole profession is well known.

This breach is not closed but relations between law teachers and the practicing members of the profession have in the last two or three decades improved immeasurably. An understanding on the part of lawyers as to what law teachers are trying to do is perceptible, and there is perceptible also a growing respect for their scholarship and for the contributions they are making to law improvement. Quite generally now the profession defers to the teacher-scholar as the interpreter of the law. The profession also has made the discovery, as evidenced in programs of the organized bar, that the best working teams on measures of law improvement are made up of lawyers, judges and law teachers. As for the law teachers, a changed attitude on their part is likewise apparent. Their interests lie in teaching and scholarship, but teaching and scholarship cannot develop in isolation. Their work must blend into that of the profession. As never before, the modern law teacher realizes he must maintain contact with the profession and its ongoing activities.

F. Legal Scholarship and Research

The story of legal education in America unfolds also the story of the evolution in America of legal scholarship. The law is a learned profession but legal scholarship, before the era of law teachers, was very nearly nonexistent. Legal scholarship centers today in the law schools. This is a known fact; yet curiously enough, little recognition is given it. Legal scholarship is the crowning achievement of legal education. It represents a tremendous contribution by law teachers to the profession and to society.

"I mentioned law," said Boswell, "as a subject on which no man could write well without practice. 'Why, Sir,' replied Johnson, "in England . . . most of our writers upon it have been in practice; though Blackstone had not been much in practice when he published his *Commentaries.* But upon the Continent, the great writers on law have not all been in practice: Grotius, indeed, was; but Pufendorf was not, Burlamaqui was not.'" Johnson, with his ever-keen faculty for discernment, was, of course, right. Had he lived to see the development of legal scholarship in America, he would have had an ample additional list of names in support of his statement.

In the history of Anglo-American legal education Blackstone was the first great teacher-scholar. He was followed in America by Kent and Story. Kent and Story, said Holdsworth, "did for your [American] law all and more than all that Blackstone did for ours."[15] Speaking in America in 1927, Holdsworth stressed the influence that law schools can exert on "the doctrines of the law. This they are able to do," said he,[16]

> "not only by the training which they give to their students, but more especially by the books upon all branches of law, and matters cognate thereto, which are written by professors to whom these schools have given the opportunity of a life devoted to legal research. Both Ames and Dicey have emphasized the fact that the advent of this professorial class has raised the standard of legal literature; and a comparison between the state of literature before the advent of such a class, and its condition today, proves that Ames and Dicey are right."

Dicey commented at length on the remarkable improvement in legal scholarship and in the literature of the law in both England and America after legal education moved

[15] *A New Discourse on the Study of the Laws* in Some Lessons from Our Legal History, 163, 186 (1928).

[16] *Ibid.*

into the universities. "Nowhere," said he,[17] "are the fruits of the movement, of which the prophet, so to speak, was Blackstone, more clearly seen than in the improvement of our legal text-books." Ames noted and stressed this transition,[18] and Thayer has left us an illuminating discussion on the subject.[19] This much is true: While opinions vary as to the content and scope of the programs of law instruction, and as to teaching methods, there is no disagreement on this, that the law teacher today holds a pre-eminent position in legal scholarship, and as the expounder and interpreter of the law.

The fields in which the legal scholar has excelled have involved the commentaries on the law, perceptive writing on legal doctrine, and scholarly legal treatises. In the main, his source materials have been the decisions of the appellate courts and the statutory law. Today, he is beginning to explore still another and highly significant area. It is an area of research that involves methods and techniques distinctly different from those with which he has had experience. It is research aimed to secure a background of facts for the solution of human conflicts and problems through law. Law is an instrument established by organized society to solve or settle these problems. But before emerging problems can be solved, whether action be by a court or a legislature, the facts that gave rise to them should be found and appraised. Thus, the first question for determination is, what are the facts that caused the problem; and, having found and appraised the facts, the next question is, what should be done to remedy the situation. Here we encounter the need for legal action. The facts them-

---

[17] *Blackstone's Commentaries*, 4 Camb. L. J. 286, 306 (1932).

[18] *The Vocation of the Law Professor* in Lectures on Legal History, 354 (1913).

[19] *The Teaching of English Law at Universities*, 9 Harv. L. Rev. 169 (1895).

selves are not legal; they are social, economic and psychological. The lawyer, of course, encounters such facts in his practice. They are the "raw facts" that give rise now to litigation and court action, and again to a need for legislation.

May it be that the lawyer and the law teacher stand today in a similar relation to legal research that the physicist did to research in physics at the beginning of the present century? The transition for the physicist has been aptly characterized in an address by P. W. Bridgman. "It is common knowledge," said he, "that since the turn of the century the physicist has passed through what amounts to an intellectual crisis forced by the discovery of experimental facts of a sort which he had not previously envisaged, and which he would not even have thought possible." But what is more compelling is Bridgman's comparison, as to complexity, between the facts of physics and the seemingly simple facts of daily life. "The world of daily life," said he, "including economics and politics, is obviously enormously more complex than the world of the physicist."

It is these facts of daily life that constitute an inviting area of study for the legal researcher. Up to now relatively little of this type of investigation that can properly be called research has been carried on. The highly revealing studies into the efficacy of penal treatment and into the causes of juvenile delinquency that have been made by Drs. Sheldon and Eleanor Glueck are illustrative of what I am attempting to describe. A recent study by Franklin M. Schultz bearing the title, "The Firm Offer Puzzle: A Study of Business Practice in the Construction Industry,"[20] and a pilot study by my colleague, A. F. Conard, made in collaboration with Robert I. Mehr, an economist, comparing costs under different systems of reparation, namely, under

[20] 19 U. Chi. L. Rev. 237 (1952).

the Federal Employers' Liability Act and the Illinois Workmen's Compensation Act,[21] offer additional illustrations. Much of the fact background on which the draft of the Uniform Commercial Code was constructed involved research of this order. Broadly conceived, we are describing research into human relations, and as such it is extremely complicated and sensitive, and its pursuit, as I have observed earlier, is costly. For the legal scholar it opens up a vast and exciting territory for research that has no beaten paths for him to travel, but this should serve only to heighten its challenge for him. For human welfare and an ordered society under law, the products of research at this level have vast potentialities.

G. LAW REVIEWS

Aside from textbooks and legal treatises, the common vehicle of legal scholarship in America is the law review. A very substantial number of the law schools publish, as a phase of the activities of the school, a law review. These reviews have two principal purposes: They are instruments of education for the students, and they are ready mediums through which legal scholars can make the results of their research available to the public. In the latter sense they serve as an aid to productivity in scholarship.

Each review ordinarily has a board of student editors made up of students who rank high in scholarship. In some schools this student board has full responsibility for the magazine. In others, the principal article section of the review and its main editorial policies are under the administration of an editor selected from the faculty; the student editors in the latter schools have charge only of the section of the review devoted to notes and comments. In either case, the student editors write the notes and com-

[21] This study, at present, is in mimeographed form.

ments. This work is highly educational for the students who participate in it, and particularly in teaching them proficiency in writing and research. A common criticism of the schools has been that, while they have opened up experiences of this sort to a limited number of high-ranking students, they have offered no comparable training of this type to students of lower rank in scholarship, the major portions of their student bodies. In a substantial measure this deficiency has been remedied through the introduction into the general curriculum of courses devoted to legal writing, legal drafting, and research and writing experience in connection with the seminars.

What is the utility of law reviews as instruments of legal education, and in a wider sphere, what is their influence? Opinions vary on these questions. Within the confines of a law school, these publications perform useful functions as incentives to productivity on the part of the members of the staff and as educational devices for students, but, as we have observed, their impact on students is limited to very small and select groups. In a more enduring sense, they are the repositories of much of the legal scholarship of the profession, and this, indeed, is a service of lasting value to legal education and to the legal profession. In the bound volumes of the law reviews the legal researcher may find scholarly articles on almost any conceivable topic of the law. There are, to be sure, numerous other legal magazines, published by the organized bar and other agencies, but the law reviews affiliated with the law schools are the principal ones devoted primarily to scholarship.

One criticism is that there are too many law reviews. Seventy-some with law-school connections are, indeed, being published in the United States. The criticism is that, since there are so many, this creates a situation in which the competition for leading articles is so intense that often, to fill the pages of the reviews, articles of little or no value to scholarship are published. There is merit in this criticism, but it is perhaps better that there be a favorable market, even though some articles of little value are published, than to have an unfavorable or restricted market with the result that some good materials may go unpublished.

Most of the law reviews published through the law schools have very limited circulations. This raises a pertinent question. Why, in a glutted market, do so many schools find it necessary or desirable to publish a review? Aside from their educational value for a limited number of students and their function as a medium through which members of law-school staffs can readily get their articles published, the answer to this question probably is a psychological one: Other schools are publishing law reviews; so must we.

The immediate influence of law reviews as current vehicles of scholarship is disappointing. They are read principally by law teachers. This consumer market is not to be disparaged, but it is a limited one. Lawyers generally do not read them. The lawyer is interested in immediate aids to him in the practice, and is restive with scholarly productions. A few lawyers do read them and the courts probably pay more attention to them than do the lawyers. Many courts are, in truth, innocent of this pursuit, but pertinent law-review articles do find their way into legal arguments in court, and some judges, and particularly some of the judges of our highest courts, quote from and cite the reviews with increasing frequency. It is a fair appraisal that the influence of the reviews in shaping the trends of the law is a growing one.

H. PROFESSIONAL STANDARDS AND ETHICS

The question as to how the law schools are to deal with the subject of legal ethics and the inculcation of professional standards and ideals in their students is still in a fluid and unsolved state. A favorable indication on this topic is that there is a growing interest in this subject on the part of the officers and some of the committees of the Association of American Law Schools. In 1951 the Association's Committee on Cooperation with the Bench and Bar made a survey to determine how many member schools were teaching courses in legal ethics.[22] This showed that only 39 schools, from a total of 87 that replied to the Committee's inquiry on this subject, were giving separate courses on legal ethics. Most of the others indicated that they were giving but casual or "incidental" attention to it. The Committee concluded its report with recommendations for closer cooperation in this field with the practicing bar and for an increased emphasis on it on the part of the teaching profession. It also recommended that the Association undertake a study of methods of instruction in this area. Currently, a special committee of the Association is exploring the feasibility of compiling and publishing in book form a selection of articles under the title, "The Legal Profession and Its Ethics." A related movement initiated early in 1952 has resulted in the setting up of a Joint Conference on the Legal Profession, the members of which were appointed by the Presidents of the American Bar Association and the Association of American Law Schools. This group has the assignment of working cooperatively within the field of professional ethics in the hope that it will be able to make a substantial contribution to the improvement of professional standards and conduct.

The Association of American Law School's Committee

---

[22] This question was also discussed in a study, to which I have previously referred, made for the Survey of the Legal Profession by Professor Elliott E. Cheatham: *The Inculcation of Professional Standards and the Functions of the Lawyer,* 21 Tenn. L. Rev. 812 (1951).

on Pre-Legal Education is now exploring an approach to the preparation for the study of law which would stress skills or mental tools rather than course content. Among the factors selected for emphasis by the Committee are insights into the understanding of the social structure, into the cultural heritage of ethics and political democracy, and into the basic human values that underlie American institutions. This approach is prompted by the increased realization of the need for adequate background for and grasp of moral values as a prerequisite to an understanding of professional responsibility.

A suggestion of broader scope was made at the 1951 meeting of the Association by its incoming President, Robert E. Mathews.[23] With the endorsement of the Executive Committee of the Association, he announced a proposal for an attack by the Association on the whole problem of training law students in the perception of moral values. He related this to an understanding of those values that underlie American democratic institutions, as well as those that bear on the functions of a lawyer in relation to his client and the court. The assumption back of this broader objective was that a substantial proportion of lawyers attain places of community and national leadership and do so for the very reason that they are lawyers; and that this in turn gives rise to responsibility on the part of the law schools to emphasize preparation for civic leadership in their programs of instruction.

I. IN PROSPECTIVE

Finally, while it is not within the assignment of a survey to divine future developments, it is congenial to our task to close this study with an appropriate quotation from one

[23] *Legal Education and Responsible Leadership,* 4 J. Legal Ed. 249 (1952), also printed in Handbook, Ass'n Am. L. Schools, 84 (1951).

of the great leaders of our day—Chief Justice Arthur T. Vanderbilt. "The function of the law schools of the second half of the twentieth century, as I envision it," said he,[24]

> "will be twofold. First, they will be responsible for training the lawyers in the future with the enlarged and enriched curriculum of which I have spoken. [He had emphasized, among other things, the teaching of international law, and the giving of greater attention to public law, criminal law and procedure, and the "how of it all."] Second, and equally important, they will also have the primary duty of leadership in the restatement and simplification of the entire body of the law and in so doing they will be giving their teaching a realism and a vitality that it could in no other way acquire. The task is a tremendous one. It is one that is crying to be done, if our civilization is to be maintained in the form and mould that every clear thinking lawyer would have it. Give our law schools the men and the material. . . . Give them the encouragement and the cooperation to which they are entitled from the bench, the bar, the government, industry and labor, and I have no doubt that they will respond effectively and enthusiastically to the greatest challenge that has ever come to American law or American lawyers."

---

[24] *The Responsibilities of Our Law Schools to the Public and the Profession*, 3 J. Legal Ed. 207, 216 (1950).

INDEX

INDEX

INDEX

INDEX

END OF VOLUME

www.ingramcontent.com/pod-product-compliance
Ingram Content Group UK Ltd.
Pitfield, Milton Keynes, MK11 3LW, UK
UKHW041623031026
15587UKWH00001B/32